march 1983

DIAGNOSIS AND ASSESSMENT IN FAMILY THERAPY

James C. Hansen, Editor
Bradford P. Keeney, Volume Editor

The Family Therapy Collections

AN ASPEN PUBLICATION ®

Aspen Systems Corporation
Rockville, Maryland
London
1983

Library of Congress Cataloging in Publication Data
Main entry under title:

Diagnosis and assessment in family therapy.

(The Family therapy collections)
Bibliography: p.
Includes index.
1. Family psychotherapy.
2. Problem family—Diagnosis.
I. Hansen, James C.   II. Keeney, Bradford P.   III. Series.
[DNLM: 1. Family therapy.   WM 430.5.P2 D536]
RC488.5.D5   1983   616.89'156   82-16456
ISBN 0-89443-603-1

Publisher: John Marozsan
Managing Editor: Margot Raphael
Printing and Manufacturing: Debbie Collins

Library of Congress Catalog Card Number: 82-6799
ISBN: 0-89443-603-1

Printed in the United States of America

1 2 3 4 5

Table of Contents

Board of Editors
(continued)

Contributors

Volume Editor

BRADFORD P. KEENEY
The Ackerman Institute for Family Therapy
New York, New York

EVAN IMBER COPPERSMITH
University of Calgary
Calgary, Alberta, Canada

LYNN HOFFMAN
The Ackerman Institute of Family
Therapy
New York, New York

STEVE DE SHAZER
Brief Family Therapy Center
Milwaukee, Wisconsin

HOWARD ARTHUR LIDDLE
Institute for Juvenile Research
University of Illinois at the
Medical Center
Chicago, Illinois

H. CHARLES FISHMAN
Family Therapy Training Center
Philadelphia Child Guidance
Clinic
Philadelphia, Pennsylvania

PHOEBE PROSKY
The Ackerman Institute for Family
Therapy
New York, New York

GEORGE S. GREENBERG
Louisiana State University
Medical School
Family Therapy Institute of
Greater New Orleans
New Orleans, Louisiana

GARY L. SANDERS
University of Calgary
Calgary, Alberta, Canada

KARL TOMM
University of Calgary
Calgary, Alberta, Canada

ANTHONY W. HEATH
Consultation for Change
Elgin, Illinois

Preface

The Family Therapy Collections is a quarterly publication designed primarily for professional practitioners. Each volume provides coverage of a single topic in family therapy in depth, with emphasis on translating theory and research into practical applications.

This volume focuses on diagnosis and assessment in family therapy. The concept of diagnosis originated in the area of medicine and meant to distinguish an illness or disease and to identify the symptoms. The concept was carried over into mental health through the influence of psychiatry; however, the model of classification of disease and treatment does not seem to apply to family therapy.

In family therapy, diagnosis denotes the prevailing condition in the family, and assessment is the process of gathering information. Although the therapist endeavors to understand each individual, assessment in family therapy concerns the patterns of interactions of those individuals. Diagnosis does not label a person or the family—it is a process. It involves an ongoing process of assessment that continues to identify behaviors and facilitate therapy over a period of time. There are numerous concepts about the diagnosing or assessing process; however, all agree it is important to understand the family's dynamics. Most theories of therapy examine similar aspects of behavior, but with variations in perspective. Assessment is an integral part of the treatment, whatever the therapist's concept of assessment may be. The assessment strategy is a necessary part of the clinical strategy.

The editor for this volume is Bradford P. Keeney, Ph.D., Director of Research, the Ackerman Institute for Family Therapy in New York City.

Dr. Keeney also teaches and consults at the Philadelphia Child Guidance Clinic, the Menninger Foundation, and the Brief Family Therapy Center of Milwaukee. He is the author of numerous essays in the field of family therapy and has completed a book, *Aesthetics of Change*, which is being published by the Guilford Press. His present work focuses on teaching the art, technique, and formal understanding of a cybernetic approach to strategic family therapy.

Dr. Keeney has selected an outstanding group of authors for this volume. Each author is a practicing family therapist as well as being involved in training. The articles present various concepts of diagnosis and assessment, but each has implications for practice.

This volume of *Collections* provides an excellent understanding of diagnosis and assessment in family therapy.

James C. Hansen
Editor

Introduction

THE CHANGE IN THERAPEUTIC FOCUS FROM AN INDIVIDUAL'S psyche to an ecology of human relationship systems has altered how we think about clinical diagnosis and assessment. Traditional psychiatric nomenclature, inseparable from a nonsystemic perspective, has difficulty finding a home in systemic approaches to family therapy. We therefore face the necessity of paradigmatic change when we formally consider diagnosis and assessment in family therapy. Following the notion that the most basic etymological meaning of diagnosis is "to know," this volume presents a variety of ways in which family therapists have attempted to articulate their ways of knowing clinical process.

As a beginning point, Howard A. Liddle, Director of the Family Systems Program at the Institute for Juvenile Research in Chicago, provides a wide-angle view of diagnosis and assessment in family therapy. His paper examines Bowenian theory, symbolic-experiential (Whitaker), structural (Minuchin), strategic (Haley), brief therapy (Mental Research Institute) and systemic (Milan associates) models of family diagnosis and assessment.

Lynn Hoffman, a senior faculty member of the Ackerman Institute for Family Therapy, makes an original contribution providing a framework for understanding systemic family therapy. Her work, closely tied to the theoretical edifice of Gregory Bateson and the clinical strategies of the Milan associates, sketches a coevolutionary way of knowing families.

H. Charles Fishman, Director of Training at the Philadelphia Child Guidance Clinic, presents a perspective of assessment through the conceptual lens of structural family therapy. He draws a distinction between structural family therapy and the work of Selvini-Palazzoli, arguing that the former works with a vastly different form of process view than the latter.

Family therapists sometimes speak of a more ecological view of assessment, suggesting that social contexts always organize symptomatic behavior. Accordingly, Evan Imber Coppersmith, Training Coordinator of the Family Therapy Program at the University of Calgary, presents a way of assessing the social contexts which encompass families, including schools, hospitals and court systems.

Karl Tomm, Director of the Family Therapy Program, Department of Psychiatry, at the University of Calgary, and his colleague, G.L. Sanders, Associate Director, provide another way of assessing families. Using a problem oriented method of record keeping, they emphasize a continuing assessment process rather than a static diagnostic classification.

Steve de Shazer, Director of the Brief Family Therapy Center in Milwaukee, Wisconsin develops the process view of diagnosis further. Using a decision tree, de Shazer demonstrates how family therapy can be organized in such a way that diagnosis and intervention are intertwined recursively.

George S. Greenberg, Director of the Family Therapy Institute of Greater New Orleans, directs attention toward the difficulties a novice family therapist encounters when he or she tries to learn family diagnosis. His contribution reminds us how different perspectives require jumps of learning.

Anthony W. Heath, Codirector of Consultation for Change, subsequently provides a way for supervisors to assess therapists. His contribution presents an efficient instrument for assessing the therapist during live supervision.

The final two papers provide different, but complementary, perspectives on the diagnostic and assessment process in family therapy. My own essay discusses an ecological way of thinking about measurement of family process. This article comments on some of the problems involved in developing a typology of family assessment and what is meant by temporally ordering one's data about a family. The final contribution by Phoebe Prosky, a senior faculty member of the Ackerman Institute for Family Therapy, is actually a parable that reminds us of the intuitive side of knowing. She argues that all digitalized, left-brain approaches to assessment and diagnosis must be augmented by the more holistic, human side of our subjective nature.

It is hoped that this collection of essays will help the clinician further understand diagnosis and assessment in family therapy. In examining these contributions, it may be wise to remember a passage from Gregory Bateson (in Ruesch & Bateson, 1968, p. 272):

> The theorist can only build his theories about what the practitioner was doing yesterday. Tomorrow the practitioner will be doing something different because of these theories.

REFERENCE

Ruesch, J., & Bateson, G., *Communication: The social matrix of psychiatry.* New York: Norton, 1968.

Bradford P. Keeney
Volume Editor

1. Diagnosis and Assessment in Family Therapy: A Comparative Analysis of Six Schools of Thought

Howard A. Liddle, Ed.D.
Director
Family Systems Program
Institute for Juvenile Research
Adjunct Assistant Professor of Psychology
Department of Psychiatry
University of Illinois at the Medical Center
Chicago, Illinois

This paper comprises some of the content from a forthcoming book by H.A. Liddle and G.W. Saba, tentatively titled *Systems of Family Therapy: A Comparative Analysis.* Belmont, Calif.: Wadsworth Publishing Company.

One

THE CONCEPT OF FAMILY DIAGNOSIS AND ASSESSMENT HAS NOT been an overly popular one in family therapy, as attention has focused mainly on the development of clinical technique. The literature that has appeared on diagnosis and assessment offers a perspective that does not take into account the different schools of thought in the field of family therapy. These contributions have been useful in categorizing the kinds of assessment instrumentation available (Cromwell, Olson, & Fournier, 1976), and the dimensions that the vast array of available instrumentation seeks to assess (Fisher, 1976). However, as the family therapy field increases its sophistication through the development of a variety of approaches, the need arises to deal with such essential therapeutic topics on a model-by-model basis. In short, diagnosis in family therapy, as in psychotherapy in general, is more useful therapeutically when one considers it within the broader context of a particular school of thought. It is insufficient to think of family diagnosis without understanding the corresponding and overarching model of therapy, which guides all aspects of any diagnostic/assessment process. The therapist's diagnostic findings and conclusions are woven into the fabric of the practiced model of therapy, since the lens of the therapy model inevitably affects his or her diagnosis and assessment. Keeney (1979) argued a related point at a broader level, pointing out the inconsistency and difficulty inherent in conducting systemically oriented diagnosis and therapy while conceptualizing a case from a linear, intrapsychic perspective.

Diagnosis might be considered a representative metaphor for the schools of family therapy. It represents the blueprint from which therapy

3

is conducted. A model-specific diagnosis provides a useful clue to an understanding of the way that approach defines and conducts the therapeutic process.

This article details—then compares and contrasts—how six major schools of family therapy define and conduct a family diagnosis/assessment:

- Bowen theory
- Symbolic-experiential (Whitaker)
- Structural (Minuchin)
- Strategic (Haley)
- Brief therapy (Mental Research Institute)
- Systemic (Milan Associates)

These models are examined along several relevant dimensions of family diagnosis and assessment.

The following questions served as the organizing framework and were posed for each model:

1. What is diagnosis? Specifically, what is diagnosed? Which domains of the family's reality are seen as most relevant to the diagnostic process? What is the relative importance of diagnosis/assessment within this school of therapy?
2. How is diagnosis/assessment conducted? What are the specific therapist skills in this regard?
3. How is the diagnosis/assessment used within the broader context of the therapy model?

BOWEN THEORY

Bowen (1978) contends that clinicians are able to view the process of diagnosis through many frames. If diagnoses were placed on a continuum of conceptual options, Bowen sees one endpoint dictating that diagnosing the identified patient would not define the family's level of functioning. The opposite end would stress the individual assessment of each family member. Bowen sees both extremes as problematic. He maintains that a midpoint stance that focuses on issues, maintaining the family projection process, is preferable. Not surprisingly, Bowen's view of assessment reflects his theoretical orientation. Bowen consistently insists that both the concept of diagnosis and the means of evaluation are dictated by the theory.

The purpose of assessment in this model is twofold:

1. to understand how the family operates, and
2. to utilize this information in devising a therapeutic plan

When any family presents itsèlf for therapy, two assumptions are made, upon which the assessment is constructed (Kerr, 1981). First, the family is operating at a universal level of activity anxiety. Second, there is a high level of emotional reactivity that impedes members' attempts to differentiate in relation to each other and to important issues.

The intensity of anxiety in symptomatic families is related to disturbances in several dimensions. These dimensions form the multifaceted picture of a family relationship system from which an assessment can be made. Some of the most relevant areas of focus are:

1. the level of differentiation of self of each family member
2. general level of functioning across as many generations as possible
3. the family's operating principles
4. the flexibility/rigidity of the system
5. the family's responsiveness to stress
6. existing family triangles
7. the function of time in the system
8. the family projection process
9. the degree of emotional cutoff from support systems, especially the extended family

Clearly, these areas of functioning reflect Bowen's conception of the family relationship system. Assessing them provides a meaningful representation of family functioning, as well as indicating a relevant therapeutic strategy.

Assessment data is gathered through what Bowen terms the "survey of the family field." This evaluation process is designed to gather a large volume of information in a brief amount of time. Formerly, this process took several hours; however, it is presently refined to a one-hour initial interview. Only the parents are present at this session, which is focused on obtaining information about the family's and couple's history. If marital discord impedes fact-gathering, then only one spouse attends, preferably the one most knowledgeable about the family. In conducting the interview, the therapist must strive to remain objective—weathering the family's emotional storm—for an accurate assessment to occur (Kerr, 1981). The therapist must also strike a balance between hearing and engaging the family and obtaining the necessary information (Guerin & Pendagast, 1976).

The structure of the interview is the same for most families, although, depending on the family, some areas need further exploration. The overall goal of the interview is to follow the entire family through time, focusing on related events in interlocking family fields; for example, how the death of a member is related to changes in various generations. As a result of the assessment the family begins to be intellectually aware of problematic functioning. The therapist, waiting until the family is more engaged, refrains from encouraging this consciousness during the initial interview. At this point, Bowen prefers to let the generation and accumulation of facts lead to the couple's awareness instead of defining the therapist's role in an interpretive way. Since families often obscure the details and facts of nodal events, the interviewing process must consist of persistent questioning and mathematical cross-checking to obtain accurate historical data (Bowen, 1978). Guerin and Pendagast (1976) suggest using a genogram to help organize the vast array of information.

Since the systematic collection of historical events is crucial to Bowen's diagnostic/assessment process, a structured interview format is recommended. The first area of exploration is the history of symptom development. An analysis is made of what the symptoms are, who has them, their onset and evolution. Exact data on the symptoms' onset and exacerbation are recorded for later examination of their relationships with important events.

The second area of investigation is the functioning of the nuclear family and how it interacts with the family of origin. A detailed history of the spouses is obtained, beginning with their first meeting. Questions are posed to the couple about their relation to extrafamilial systems, sources of stress, marital conflicts, and physical illnesses. Each spouse's vocational, educational, and health histories are taken, as is an estimate of each of their children's present level of functioning. The family's living conditions and significant geographic moves are recorded as well. Bowen (1978) believes that the multigenerational family projection process is a significant source of assessment data, which can be understood by requesting the mother to relate her fantasies and expectations before and after the birth of her children. Next, the extended family of each spouse is explored. Either spouse may present first. Assessed areas include the emotional functioning of parents and siblings, the spouse's sibling position, location of family of origin, and the degree of emotional cutoff from the family. Health, educational, occupational, and marital histories of the spouses' parents and siblings are taken. Dates of major events are noted.

The final stage of the interview defines what the family will work on in therapy. Kerr suggests helping the family defocus the symptom, but define its emotional atmosphere. The emphasis is on everyone's contribution to family anxiety and the need for commitment toward collaborative work for change (Kerr, 1981).

The data gathered from this interview are not seen independently but collectively, and present an overall pattern of family functioning. For example, a family with a low level of differentiation will have a greater frequency and intensity of related events, such as the death of a spouse and consequent symptom formation. Or, the rapidity of symptom development can identify the level of dysfunction as well as prognosis. For instance, a rapidly developing problem is often related to difficulties in the extended family and is more easily resolved than a symptom resulting from a gradual building of tension in the more immediate family of procreation (Bowen, 1978).

The Bowen method of diagnosis and evaluation is strongly based on self-report data and subsequent analysis of overall historical patterns of family functioning. The stress on development and appreciation of multiple generations, the emphasis on obtaining cognitive data, and restraint of affect during the assessment all reflect the assumptions of the Bowen model of family treatment.

SYMBOLIC-EXPERIENTIAL THERAPY

For some time, it has been difficult to discern the theoretical components of Carl Whitaker's highly personal, idiosyncratic brand of therapy. Whitaker himself has not always aided discernment; at times he described his approach as a nontechnical model of family therapy (Whitaker, 1976). Presented in this caricatured form, his position alerted therapists to the dangers of an overreliance on theory to the exclusion of the person of the therapist. Gradually, however, Whitaker's therapy has become more understandable, thanks largely to his coauthored publications with former trainees such as Gus Napier (Napier & Whitaker, 1978); David Keith (Keith & Whitaker, 1981); and others (Neill & Kniskern, 1982). This succeeding generation of Whitaker-styled therapists has extrapolated the conceptual principles and reproducible elements of Whitaker's therapy. These efforts have not only served to translate and standardize certain idiosyncrasies of the originator; they have added new dimensions to the model. The result is not so much a codification of Whitaker's style as a move in the direction of a true model of therapy that can transcend the personal charisma of its "Great Original" (Hoffman, 1981).

A key aspect in the diagnostic process, as in the therapy model itself, is the therapist's use of self—"We always read our own responses in the assessment" (Keith & Whitaker, 1981, p. 198). The therapist's anxiety level, physical sensations (muscle tightness, depersonalization feelings), and primary process-like associations are, according to this model, all valid channels of diagnostic information. In this sense, there is significant trust placed in the therapist's intuitive processes. For Whitaker, contrary to most other schools, diagnosis is primarily a "right-brain" (analogic vs. digital) operation. The therapist must be free to reveal those aspects of self that focus on the symbolic and metaphoric spheres of the family's existence. This school argues that the family should not affectively expose itself unless the therapist is free to do the same.

Beyond the crucial importance of a therapist's use of self in diagnosis in the symbolic-experiential approach lies the more recently developed diagnostic schema, a framework with several key aspects. The concept of pathology itself serves as an organizing principle: "Our general orientation toward pathological functioning is related to the concept of craziness" (Keith & Whitaker, 1981, p. 194). Dysfunction, however, is redefined in terms other than those of sickness. Complementary aspects of an individual's symptom are seen as important to understand and directly establish. For Whitaker, just as every "black sheep" is balanced by the existence of a "white knight," underfunctioning (symptoms) is often obscured and complemented by an overfunctioning, overcompetent family member.

Although the symbolic-experiential diagnostic system is basically informal, some guidelines have been developed. At the most basic level, the therapist should assess the quality of intimacy and the family's sense of themselves as a viable, ongoing, ever changing, yet constant unit. In Keith and Whitaker's words:

> We try to evaluate the interactional aspects of the two cultures
> of the families of origin and the situational dynamics in the

present, as well as historical residuals from situational stress, whether physical illness, death of family members, divorce or other shifts in family function. We look for ghost members, symbiotic interactions across generations. In the early part of therapy, assessment is mainly behavioral and interpersonal. After the family members adopt the assumption of themselves as a biologically cohesive unit, we work backwards toward the intrapsychic world. The separation of intrapsychic, behavioral, and interpersonal is regarded as arbitrary. It is useful semantically and for theoretical examination but in reality there is no difference. (1981, p. 198)

Along this same stage-oriented dimension, Whitaker has long considered the "battle for structure" and "battle for initiative" as two early phases of therapy that can clarify much about the family's functioning. In the former stage, the therapist must notice the ways the family will test the therapist, showing its natural resistance to change (e.g., members refusing to come in, or arguments about the nature, format, or fee of therapy). The therapist must firmly establish therapy's ground rules, and from this perspective, if the therapist can take responsibility for the conduct of the therapy, the family can take charge of their lives. The "battle for initiative" stage has diagnostic assessment value as well. This phase requires the family to take its own responsibility for change and not to rely on the therapist's healing magic. In this stage, the natural resources in the family, along with the ways in which it is currently dysfunctioning, become patently clear to the therapist and family. It is a time where the therapist's role becomes less central as he observes the ways family members relate to each other and begin their struggle to find the initiating energy that begins change.

Uniquely, the dimension of *desperateness* is both an assessment factor and prognostic indicator in the symbolic-experiential approach. Pragmatically, the therapist determines the degree to which a family feels itself to be desperately in need of change. The therapist also assesses what have been called the *universals* of family life in our culture. The therapist makes multiple process assumptions about families and how they work (fathers as more peripheral, mothers as gate-keepers, for example). This assessment provides constant, projective test-like stimuli to which the family can respond.

An examination of the goals of a symbolic-experiential family therapy yields an extrapolated list of questions for the therapist to ask about the family's functioning (Keith & Whitaker, 1981, p. 200).

1. To what degree can this family tolerate the natural interpersonal stress of family life?
2. To what degree does the family possess a family nationalism—a team spirit or family esprit de corps?
3. To what degree is the family appropriately or inappropriately linked with at least three generations of the extended family?
4. What are the boundaries of this family, and to what degree are the generations separate, yet able to flexibly handle different family roles and functions?
5. To what degree can the family play and spontaneously have fun together?
6. To what degree can the family tolerate the constant cycle of separation and rejoining existent in all family life?
7. To what degree are "creative forces" tolerated in the family? To what degree is each family member free to "be more of who he/she is, with . . . access to him/herself"?

Lastly, Keith and Whitaker offer a three-pronged caveat to therapists interested in making a family diagnosis.

> The first is that our language is not structured to describe process. The result is that a diagnosis may have iatrogenic effects on the life of the family by reifying the problems. The second is that diagnostic terms are extended metaphors, and attempt to make one kind of reality conform to another kind of reality. The third problem is that each family has a private culture and language system to which the therapist has only partial access. In our view therapy is the family's trip. We are like guides. The diagnostic process may be crippling to the family and/or mystifying. (Keith & Whitaker, 1981, p. 197)

Thus, any therapeutic activity that might interfere with the therapist–family relationship—the sine qua non of the model—is certainly to be avoided. The therapist, too, is a participant–observer, and as such is forever subjective in his or her perceptions. This subjectivity, which is given a negative valence with some of the other models (Bowen, Milan), is in the symbolic-experiential approach framed as an inevitability and used as an essential therapeutic ingredient.

STRUCTURAL FAMILY THERAPY

From its earliest days of development and refinement into a theory of therapy, structural family therapy has placed considerable emphasis on the concept of a therapist's careful assessment of a family's interactional patterns and organization. In the Wiltwick Project, Minuchin and his colleagues struggled to define the transactional qualities of families that produced severely acting out delinquents (Minuchin, Montalvo, Guerney, Rosman, & Schumer, 1969). They then generated what was to eventually become a basic typology for assessing the preferred transactional styles of all families—the enmeshed/disengaged continuum. The Psychosomatic Project continued in this model-building way by basing a treatment model on the carefully observed characteristics of the psychosomatic families (Minuchin, Rosman, & Baker, 1978). The Heroin Addicts and Families Project similarly followed this path. In this case a structural-strategic model based upon an interactional typology of family themes and patterns (Stanton & Todd, 1982) was applied.

Several key concepts are essential to a structural diagnosis of the family. The idea of the family moving through predictable developmental crises in its life is central to both the assessment and therapy process. Minuchin defines the family as an open sociocultural system in transformation. This conception describes the family's necessity to adapt flexibly to unforeseen external and internal developmental demands for change. Symptoms tend to occur most at these developmental transition points, and it is at this evolutionary level of analysis that much of a structural assessment occurs. Making this assessment, however, requires a more specific framework—in this case, a structural or organizational framework within which family phenomena can be charted.

Family structure is thought of as the invisible set of functional demands that organize the ways in which family members interact (Minuchin, 1974). The structure is, in essence, the sum of the rules of interaction patterns. Families maintain themselves by generic or universal rules, such as hierarchy, as well as by individualized rules. The therapist probes the family structure through an investigation of these generic and individualized or idiosyncratic rules on several dimensions of family functioning:

- proximity and distance
- boundaries
- subsystems functioning
- the family's developmental stage

The proximity and distance dimension relates to the degree to which family members can obtain both belonging (closeness) and individuation (separateness). The need for psychological and physical closeness and distance is a basic one in all families. It is on this core dimension of family life that the therapist conducts an important part of his assessment.

Families differentiate and carry out their basic functions partly because of their organization into subsystems, which are usually delineated according to age, interest, function, and gender. The parental, marital, sibling, and intergenerational subsystems are the most common units of assessment. It is essential for the therapist to understand the functions of the various subsystems. In this sense the importance of the therapist's conceptual ability is obvious within structural therapy. The therapist has several maps or conceptual overlays available. In addition to the family life cycle and subsystem function schemas for assessment, the therapist also has available knowledge of how certain family forms yield predictable structures and processes. In *Family Therapy Techniques,* Munuchin and Fishman (1981) detail six of these forms, useful in guiding a therapist's diagnostic formulations. These include:

- families with two people
- three-generational structures
- large families
- families with fluctuating membership
- stepparent families

For the family's subsystems to be effective in carrying out their psychosocial tasks, they must be free from interference from other subsystems. Minuchin's concept of boundaries applies here. Boundaries, dealing with subsystems membership, are defined as the rules governing participation by family members. They are the glue that holds the family structure together. Boundaries, however, do not only serve exclusionary functions. They must also permit contact among members of the subsystems and others in the family. Enmeshed and disengaged are two extremes of boundary functioning; the former presents a poorly differentiated organization (diffuse boundaries) and the latter a structure with rigid boundaries. They are seen as preferred transactional styles and are thought of as an approximate framework for a therapist's assessment of boundary functioning. The therapist is encouraged to develop hypotheses about structure from his or her first exposure to the family (intake information and telephone conversations). This information should stimulate the therapist to quickly begin to think about the possibility of certain family shapes and problem areas. This process assists in organizing the initial interview.

Crucial to the assessment process in the structural school is the therapist's use of self. The therapist's own style and way of relating create a context where relevant interactional phenomena can be experienced and observed. Diagnosis then is experientially based: "the therapist . . . must let himself be pulled and pushed by the system in order to experience its characteristics" (Minuchin & Fishman, 1981, p. 4). The therapist, then, is the instrument of interactional diagnosis and change and it is this flexible use of self that makes therapy succeed. In this regard, the therapist ". . . must become comfortable with different levels of involvement" (Minuchin & Fishman, 1981, p. 31). In the joining process, the therapist sometimes becomes intentionally inducted into the ebb and flow of the family drama, using this proximate position to experience some of the family's transactions in addition to the structure the members themselves regularly encounter. From a less close position, the therapist tracks the family process as another means of family assessment. The therapist pays particular attention to his or her own reactions to the family and the way their behaviors organize his or her actions. The therapist observes, for example, whether he or she talks mostly to one member and ignores others.

Another major principle in the structural view of assessment is that of enactment. An understanding of this principle helps to clarify the structural position on diagnosis/assessment. Enactment is not only a tool that will reveal the family's interactional deficits, but it is also construed as a means of creating a context from which new behaviors can emerge.

> Instead of taking a history, the therapist addresses himself to bringing areas that the family has framed as relevant into the session. He assumes that since the family is dysfunctional only in certain areas, paying attention to these particular areas will provide insight into the central family dynamics. The assump-

tion is that the family structure becomes manifest in these transactions and that the therapist will therefore catch a glimpse of
the rules that govern transactional patterns in the family. Problems as well as alternatives thus become available in the present
and in relation to the therapist. (Minuchin & Fishman, 1981, p.
80)

In this sense one observes the interdependence of diagnosis and therapy
or perhaps more precisely, the nonrigid boundary between the two.

From this position, the myth of the therapist as an objective observer
"trying to obtain an accurate reporting of what is 'really' there" (Minuchin & Fishman, 1981, p. 80) quickly vanishes. The therapist actively
participates in the creation of the therapeutic reality realizing that
". . . the act of observation influences the material observed"; thus we
". . . are always dealing in approximates and probable realities" (Minuchin & Fishman, 1981, p. 80). In this sense, the therapist does not find it
necessary to wait for a long period before intervening. He or she does not
hold out until a more comprehensive view of the family's reality is
obtained. The structural position holds that a therapist can obtain a valid
diagnostic profile, and therefore have enough data to intervene, on the
basis of the isomorphic transactions in the family structure. Isomorphs are
interactions that are dissimilar in content but similar in form at a deeper
level (*iso*=equivalent; *morphs*=structures). Thus the therapist's assessment might include a number of apparently different areas of content.
The task is to understand the ways in which they are isomorphically
related at a structural-interactional level.

In summary, the diagnosis/assessment process in structural family therapy has several central interlocking principles:

- the themes of the family's developmental level
- how issues of proximity and distance get negotiated
- the interdependent functioning of a family's subsystems
- boundary maintenance
- the overarching concept of family structure

From this perspective the therapist is not an objective bystander who
holds a clipboard and draws family maps, but is an acting and reacting
member of the system, capable of operating from proximate *and* disengaged positions. The therapist realizes that a true, comprehensive and

final perspective on the family's total reality is impossible. The therapist is thus allowed to work with these partial constructs, which the therapist helps to create. The therapist uses this experientially gathered data to generate hypotheses about the family. These hypotheses serve as guides for the therapist, yet are tentative conclusions and subject to change throughout the course of therapy. Assessment thus becomes an ongoing process. It should be seen interdependently and in oscillation with one's interventions. In structural therapy, diagnosis becomes the result of the therapist's interventions.

STRATEGIC THERAPY

The strategic approach of Jay Haley emanates from the theoretical roots of Gregory Bateson and the clinical artistry of Milton Erickson, both significant figures in Haley's development. Both traditions taught Haley the importance of a keen observational ability—Bateson in the anthropological sense, and Erickson in the way a hypnotist reads cues from patients.

In the strictest sense, Haley sees traditional diagnostic classification as harmful to the therapeutic enterprise, since "the way one labels a human dilemma can crystallize a problem and make it chronic" (Haley, 1976, p. 3). Since Haley was indirectly (through Don D. Jackson), but significantly influenced by Harry Stack Sullivan, his subscription to Sullivan's participant-observer concept should not be surprising. In Haley's terms, the therapist and his professional colleagues can be defined as part of the problem therapy seeks to change. Initial assessment at the broader extra-familial level is required to understand how involved professionals have defined and treated (with medication and hospitalization) the patient and family. Haley's assessment of the wider social unit is therefore an important initial step in the first phase of therapy.

Haley clearly differentiates between diagnosis for institutional reasons and diagnosis for therapy purposes. He sees individual diagnostic categories to be irrelevant to therapy and potentially harmful to the conceptualization ability of the therapist. For Haley

> . . . the best diagnosis *for therapy* is one that allows the social group to respond to attempts to bring about change. A therapist must intervene with a therapeutic act to gather diagnostic infor-

mation for therapy, so it is best to begin with everyone involved because change will involve everyone. (Haley, 1976, p. 12)

At the level of the family unit, assessment focuses on several key dimensions, including interactional sequences and the hierarchical organization of the family. Assessment occurs in relation to the presenting problem or symptom, the alleviation of which constitutes successful therapy in this model. The assessment dimensions of sequence and hierarchy might best be treated within the context of Haley's formula for an initial interview. It is in this crucial phase of therapy that the therapist formulates the presenting problem in ways which will maximize its dissolution. For Haley, "If therapy is to end properly, it must begin properly—by negotiating a solvable problem and discovering the social situation that makes the problem necessary" (Haley, 1976, p. 9).

To gain the most useful diagnostic information, Haley recommends beginning therapy with a structured, stage-specific first interview, the outline of which is presented below.

Although the focus at the initial, *social stage* phase is on the greeting of the family and the creation of a cordial, comfortable context, several areas of assessment are delineated in this stage. The therapist notes the parent–child relations (e.g., discipline issues, mood), the relationship between parents or other adults who bring the children (such as mother and grandmother) in terms of their agreement about how to deal with the child, the ways in which family members deal with the therapist (e.g., coalition building), and nonverbal cues such as the spatial/seating arrangement. The therapist does not comment on these observations, but keeps them as partial data to help formulate beginning hypotheses about the family organization.

In the *problem stage*, the therapist makes the initial inquiry about all of the family members' perceptions of the presenting problem. The therapist listens metaphorically and digitally—for both relationship messages and content descriptions.

> When listening to people talk about the problem, the therapist should keep in mind that they are not only telling him facts and opinions but also are saying things indirectly that cannot be said directly. (Haley, 1976, p. 31)

The therapist is also careful to note how the problem is framed by family members—do they see it as one person's difficulty or as an interactional problem in which they are involved? At this stage the therapist does not offer interpretations or share observations of the family's interaction. The goal of this phase is to elicit individual perspectives on the presenting problem.

The second step in asking about the problem overcomes some of the problems with self-report data. The *interaction stage* moves the therapist from a central posture toward a position where family members are organized to discuss the problem with each other, especially in terms of facilitating their disagreements.

Further, the therapist moves past this conversational level and should try at this stage to bring the problem directly into the room.

> For example, if a child deliberately bangs his head, he can be asked to do so. The family will show how it responds. If a child sets fires, he can set one (in a metal ashtray) so that the knowledge he has of how to handle matches as well as the response of everyone is clarified . . . If a wife complains and is depressed, she may be asked to behave that way and then everyone can show how they respond. (Haley, 1976, p. 38)

Thus the family's typical ways of responding and interacting can be assessed by moving the presenting problem into the room. Doing so gives the therapist a new and valuable source of data, not possible when individual self-reports are presented serially. Haley advises observation of these transpersonal phenomena with a framework that emphasizes organization and sequence. He believes that to be organized means that a system follows patterned, redundant ways of behaving and exists in a hierarchy, that is, a structure where differential levels of status or power exist. Haley's conviction of the importance of assessing the hierarchical organization of a family is related to his theory of dysfunction.

> When an individual shows symptoms, the organization has a hierarchical arrangement that is confused. It may be confused by being ambiguous so that no one quite knows who is his peer and who is his superior. It may also be confused because a member at one level of the hierarchy consistently forms a coalition against a peer with a member at another level, thus violating the basic rules of organization. (Haley, 1976, p. 102)

In these situations, the therapist defines these struggles as efforts to clarify or to work out the positions in the organizational hierarchy. Thus in the assessment phase, a need exists to map out the hierarchic structure. Haley defines structure not in static terms, but in a process-oriented way, as repeating acts among people. Haley, in the Batesonian tradition, defines sequences as essentially circular processes or repeating cycles. In terms of a therapist's assessment, these sequences must first be charted from both self-reports and direct observation through enactment of the problem, and then changed by the therapist's intervening in such a way that the problem cannot continue.

Directives are designed to fit the idiosyncratic needs of the family and the presenting problem. Directives are based upon a careful assessment of organization and sequence. The therapist must assess the particular style and language of the family and be sure to frame the directives in these terms. Again, the observational skills of the therapist are crucial.

If the family members emphasize doing things in an orderly, logical manner, the task offered to them should be an orderly, logical task . . . If they form a casual, disorderly household, a casual framework for the task may be more appropriate. (Haley, 1976, p. 56)

In summary, the therapist is sensitive to the hierarchic organization of the family, assessing this dimension first along generational lines. In this regard, coalitions across generations are especially common in dysfunctional families. The therapist's assessment task here is to define this organizational configuration in structural terms, which includes a process-oriented tracking of the interactional sequences which perpetuate the hierarchical and organizational problems. Haley reminds therapists of the broader contextual factors involved in the maintenance of individual and family problems, and advises that these domains be grist for the therapist's assessment efforts. Assessment for Haley does not mean construing symptoms only in strict behavioral terms, but regarding them as relationship and social context metaphors. In this strategic approach, directives are the key therapy technique. Haley advises us to use the feedback (compliance, noncompliance) from these directives as further useful diagnostic data, thereby treating assessment as a continuous, not a stage-specific therapeutic task.

BRIEF THERAPY

The brief therapy model of the Mental Research Institute (MRI) group was codified with the publication of "Brief Therapy: Focused Problem

Resolution" in 1974 and with their book *Change: Principles of Problem Formation and Resolution* by Watzlawick, Weakland, and Fisch, published later that year. The model has most recently been described in terms of its parsimony or economy of technique. In Hoffman's (1981) words,

> If a clinician is successful in identifying the sequence of which the symptom is a vital part, a very small change can presumably be pinpointed accurately enough to have a wide reaching effect. (p. 213)

This focus on observable, repeating, mutually causative and reinforcing cycles of interaction is the essence of the brief therapy model's diagnostic process. The approach is sensitive to the ways in which normal life difficulties escalate into problems through mishandling (over- or under-emphasis). The assessment focus is on how people conceptualize their problems, what specifically they try to do to solve them, and who (other than the symptomatic individual) is involved in maintaining the cycles of attempted remediation.

Communication and cybernetic theory are important conceptual underpinnings of MRI therapy. The theoretical core of brief therapy includes these concepts:

- complementary (exchange of different types of behavior) versus symmetrical (exchange of like kinds of behavior) relationships
- rules and redundancies in relationships
- analogic and digital, and report (content) and command (relationship) aspects of communication

The text *Pragmatics of Human Communication* (Watzlawick, Jackson, & Beavin, 1967) represents the epistemological foundation of the MRI school.

With this theoretical emphasis, it can easily be seen how therapists of this persuasion consistently conceive of problems in terms of *rule-governed systems of interaction that repeat over time*. In this regard, the role of history is not important in the MRI paradigm. The therapist's detective work is more anthropologic than historic, as *current* redundant patterns of interaction are uncovered and interrupted. Symptoms are most likely to occur when some life change or transition is required—the seasons of birth, death, marriage, divorce, and the like. The family life cycle has some, but not major, theoretical relevance to the MRI school.

The key to the approach remains, as Weakland (1976) has termed it, the therapist's understanding of the client's bad handling of the problem. Three major types of mishandling are:

1. when action is necessary but is not taken (underemphasis and denial)
2. when action is taken when it should not be (overemphasis and overreaction, often related to utopian expectations)
3. when action is taken at the incorrect level (attempted solutions *become* the problem)

The therapist's role in diagnosis moves beyond categorization and requires a close tracking of the client's report of the problem. Questions pertaining to the *why* aspects of human functioning are not relevant to the diagnostic and treatment process. The therapist investigates *what* is happening in the client's systems of interaction—how the problem is framed or understood, and who else (especially those actively responding to the problem) is involved with the client. Vague, general responses are not useful. The therapist seeks self-report data that are highly specific, descriptive, and oriented toward sequences of behavior.

Two additional aspects of the MRI model have particular relevance to the diagnostic process. Two questions are posed at the outset of therapy in order for the approach to be successfully implemented. First, the therapist determines who the "customer" for therapy is. The customer is the main client for treatment—the person who most wants a definitive change in the stated problem. This need not be the identified patient or the person initiating therapy but is simply the person (or persons) most overtly concerned or affected by the problem. (There may be more than one customer.) The brief therapy approach views systemic change to be more likely and resistance lower when the therapist works through the chief complainant(s). As Weakland has said, "If one takes the idea of interaction in systems seriously, it follows that effective intervention can be made through any member of the system" (1976, p. 126). From this perspective, diagnosis is not necessarily obtained by having all family members present for therapy but rather lies in the therapist's capacity to *conceptualize interactionally*—in terms of the transactions that perpetuate problem maintenance.

The second crucial assessment question at the start of therapy attends to the customer's or client's world view, the composite of values, hopes, fears, prejudices, and expectations that make up any individual. The MRI model encapsulates information from these areas with the question: what is the client's *language*? This query seeks to

> . . . determine what approach would appeal most to the particular patient—to observe where he lives and meet this need, whether it is to believe in the magical, to defeat the expert, to be a caretaker of someone, to face a challenge, or whatever. (Watzlawick & Weakland, 1977, p. 288)

This assessment ascertains the client's idiosyncratic characteristics and motivational variables, and defines them as potential entry points and levers for change.

In sum, assessment in brief therapy consists of the therapist's ability to obtain a clear, interactionally oriented picture of the client's and others' description of the problem, and the attempted solutions and reactions to it. This typically occurs during the first or second session, and until these descriptive data are collected, no therapeutic directives are given. These prescriptions are based precisely on the assessment data, and are designed and framed according to the idiosyncrasies of the particular context. The directives are intended to interdict the vicious cycles of problem perpetuation. They create feedback loops of responding that are more positive, and are themselves prone to repetition and self-reinforcement.

SYSTEMIC THERAPY

Referred to as the systemic model of family therapy (Hoffman, 1981), the approach of the Milan Associates has achieved enormous popularity and professional attention. Their approach has evolved significantly since publication of their first book, *Paradox and Counterparadox,* in 1978. They have gradually added to and refined their basic model in a series of published papers appearing in diverse sources (Selvini Palazzoli, Cecchin, Prata, & Boscolo, 1978a, 1978b, 1980a, 1980b, 1980c).

The approach of Selvini Palazzoli et al. has been known primarily as one of the strategic approaches to family therapy (although there is some controversy about this classification). The Milan model emphasizes a prescriptive and paradoxical approach based upon a systemic understanding of the family. This view seeks to connect the pieces of a family's behavior in order to compose a unified, interrelated whole. Many professionals, however, in their understanding and implementation of this approach have emphasized the often dramatic interventions of the Milan model—the systemic prescriptions or therapeutic binds—rather than the procedures designed to make the interventions possible. An analogy might be an emphasis on the thrilling conclusion to a detective story rather than on understanding the tedious, detail-oriented background work needed to solve the mystery. The Milan team has become expert at this latter kind of therapeutic activity, which is essential to their approach.

The Milan group construes the referral process as often containing information crucial to an understanding of the family's dilemma. In their paper "The Problem of the Referring Person" (Selvini Palazzoli, et al., 1980b), they comprehensively detail the ways in which the referral source, although well intentioned, serves to help maintain the family's problems. Because referral sources often serve as an agent of homeostasis rather than change, the initial assessment step in the Milan approach involves not only the family system, but the unit of the family *plus* the referring agency/person. Therapists are advised to collect data on the referral process systematically, especially in terms of the relationship history between the family and the referring professional.

In addition to this emphasis on the extrafamilial or macrosystems that can influence a family's situation, the Milan model, of course, has also been concerned with developing useful ways of assessing the family's processes and organization.

"Hypothesizing, Circularity, Neutrality: Three Guidelines for the Conductor of the Session" (Selvini Palazzoli et al., 1980a) is the authors' most useful work for the kind of assessment that can lead to a systemic prescription that can account for the many, interlocking elements of family behavior. Central to this assessment process is the development of a hypothesis about the family's relational patterns, which are seen as a starting point for the therapist's work. Hypotheses are defined as suppositions about the family's functioning that are "tentatively accepted to provide a basis for further investigation" (Selvini Palazzoli et al., 1980a, p. 5).

Further, hypotheses are useful because of the feedback they can elicit. The therapist, through a trial and error process of making assumptions (which grow into hypotheses), receives corrective feedback from the family on the accuracy of these assumptions. In this manner, hypotheses encourage an exploration of certain nodal aspects of a family's life, and serve as productive organizers for a therapist during a session. Selvini Palazzoli et al. believe hypothesizing and checking for the veracity of the hypotheses is a key aspect in keeping the therapist active, and more importantly, in a position which is *meta* to the family (less amenable to the system's inductive power).

The best hypotheses are "systemic"; that is, they include all components of the family's relational system and provide concrete ideas about how the pieces of the family's puzzle interrelate. In the words of Selvini Palazzoli et al. (1980a), it gives "a supposition of the total relational function of the family" (p. 6). The hypotheses are joined on the basis of an examination of referral dynamics, information derived from the universal aspects of the particular family's experience, and from information on the specific, idiosyncratic interactional patterns of the family.

Over the years the Milan team strove to model its thinking and therapy after the writings of Bateson, an epistemological mentor to many in the family therapy field. The key concepts are (1) relationship (the inaccuracy of thinking only in terms of discrete things vs. interrelationships) and (2) circularity (the therapist's capacity to, in the words of Selvini Palazzoli, 1980a, p. 8, "conduct his investigation on the basis of feedback from the family in response to the information he solicits about relationships"). For the Milan team two fundamental Batesonian principles must be kept in mind during the assessment process. They are:

1. Information is a difference.
2. Difference is a relationship (or a change in the relationship).

Relationships and organization are diagnosed through a process Selvini Palazzoli et al. call circular questioning:

> Every member of the family is invited to tell us how he sees the relationship between two other members of the family. Here we are dealing with the investigation of a dyadic relationship as it is seen by a third person. (1980a, p. 8)

Several methods are described to elicit this useful relationship information. Also referred to as the "gossiping in the presence of others" technique, circular questioning explores the complex series of triadic relationships and perceptions of relationships in a systematic way. The two major areas of inquiry include:

1. Questions posed in terms of eliciting differences. (Example: the therapist to the father: who is more attached to his mother, Robert or Louis?)
2. Questions posed in terms of specific interactive behavior in specific situations. (Example: the therapist to a sibling in a family of four: when your brother loses his temper with your mother, what does your father do, and how does your mother react to what he does or does not do? What do you do?'')

The therapist thus elicits and attends not only to the self-report data generated by these difference-seeking questions but also to the in-session reactions to this elicitation.

The final component essential to the assessment process concerns the stance of the therapist. Referring to it as *neutrality,* Selvini Palazzoli et al. (1980a) describe this posture as the "specific pragmatic effect that his [the therapist's] total behavior during the session exerts on the family" (p. 11). The Milan group strives to keep the therapist out of coalitions and alliances with family members and the group further deemphasizes the role of a therapist's power, charisma, and personality. The therapist's role is to provoke feedback and collect information via the circular questioning method. Selvini Palazzoli et al. (1980a) link this therapeutic posture with therapeutic outcome, believing that the therapist "can be effective only to the extent that he is able to obtain and maintain a different level (metalevel) from that of the family" (p. 11).

Hoffman (1981), often serving as a model translator for the Milan group, has articulated several advantageous outcomes of their circular questioning.

> First of all such questions make people stop and think, rather than react in a stereotyped way . . . Second, these questions cut into escalations and fights . . . And, third, they seem to trigger more of the same kind of "difference" thinking, which is essentially circular because it introduces the idea of links made up of shifting perspectives. (p. 301)

COMPARATIVE ANALYSIS

This section briefly highlights the similarities and differences among the six models of family therapy. The comparative analysis serves as a beginning framework for those interested in understanding the points of convergence and divergence among the approaches. For a summary of this material, see Table 1-1.

Table 1-1   Comparative Outline of Diagnosis/Assessment in Six Models of Family Therapy

Models	Dimensions of Diagnosis/Assessment (D/A)		
	Relevant concepts	*Methods/Role of therapist*	*D/A within the therapy model*
Bowen Theory	• family's anxiety level and emotional reactivity • degree of differentiation of self of each family member • general level of functioning across the generations • family projection process • emphasis on triadic vs. dyadic relationships • flexibility–rigidity • family's responsiveness to stress • family's operating principles	• is objective, detached from family emotional system • collects data from parents on: history of symptoms development, functioning of nuclear family and its interaction with family of origin, and the extended family of each spouse • uses genogram to organize data	• differentiation of self from family of origin as a goal is only possible after a careful assessment of the historical context of the family
Systemic Therapy: Milan Associates	• systemic understanding— how the historical and current pieces of the family puzzle fit	• uses circular questioning— asking one person about two others: emphasis on difference	• the data-gathering, neutral stance of the therapist permits useful interactional data (feed-

(continues)

Table 1-1 continued

	Dimensions of Diagnosis/Assessment (D/A)		
Models	Relevant concepts	Methods/Role of therapist	D/A within the therapy model
	• circular causality—interdependent and complementary nature of symptoms • information is a "difference" in relationship • referral process and contextual factors	• generates family members reactions to and perceptions of symptoms • hypothesizing organizes therapist's behavior, sensitivity to feedback from family regarding hypotheses • neutrality prescribes a stance at an objective, nonaligned meta-level	back) and self-report information to emerge • systemic hypothesis is based on circular causality • therapist prescribes rituals, tasks, and paradoxical prescriptions
Symbolic-Experiential: Whitaker	• complementarity of symptoms • focus on analogic, metaphoric, symbolic • degree of separateness-connectedness • intergenerational themes • growthful, creative aspects of symptoms • scapegoat's anxiety relieving function • desperateness as a readiness factor in change • therapeutic relationship	• therapeutic use of self: reading awareness of own responses, self-disclosure • assesses family's ability to tolerate natural interpersonal stress of family life; degree of family nationalism (esprit de corps); ability to play; have role flexibility; toleration of deviance (creativity)	• the D/A process is seen as potentially stultifying and impinging on therapeutic spontaneity and relationship • battle for structure and for initiative phases highly diagnostic/prognostic • therapist pushes for expansion of self, flexibility of roles

(continues)

Table 1-1 continued

| | Dimensions of Diagnosis/Assessment (D/A) | | |
Models	Relevant concepts	Methods/Role of therapist	D/A within the therapy model
Structural: Minuchin	• focuses on structure, organization of the family, subsystems, boundaries, hierarchy, alliances, coalitions, family life cycle, enmeshed-disengaged continuum as a guide • D/A an active, experiential process; diagnosis seen as a result of therapists' interventions • isomorphs and partial constructs of reality • wider social unit • search for strengths	• uses self as an instrument/a therapeutic probe • seeks interactional data from self-report and in-session sequences (enactment) • therapist identifies the presenting problem within the structures sequences and surrounding context • D/A and intervention as arbitrarily divided • D/A as on-going, based on continual feedback	• through a continual, experiential reading of the family structure (made up of repeating patterns), therapist uses self to challenge and realign/restructure relationships • therapist accesses aspects of family members that are available but unused • new relational realities become self-reinforcing
Strategic: Haley	• presenting problem focus, ahistoric, symptoms as relationship metaphors, as adaptive in relationships • symptoms conceptualized analogically, worked with digitally • family life cycle, transition points	• structured initial interview • data generated from self-report and in-session sequences promoted by therapist • observational skills important • use of feedback • language of the family as having	• therapist solves presenting problems in the social contexts in which they exist through directives (straightforward and paradoxical) designed to interrupt the patterned sequences and

(continues)

Table 1-1 continued

	Dimensions of Diagnosis/Assessment (D/A)		
Models	Relevant concepts	Methods/Role of therapist	D/A within the therapy model
	• sequences of behavior, hierarchical organization • wider social unit • traditional diagnoses crystallize problems	assessment value • flexibility vs. standardization of methods	realign the hierarchic incongruities of the malfunctioning organization • creation of greater complexity in the family system
Brief Therapy: MRI	• ahistoric, symptom-focused • emphasizes sequences of observable interactions, seen as mutually causative and reinforcing (circular causality) • symptoms seen as the result of mishandling of problems—the attempted solution is the problem (over- and underemphasis) • symptoms at life's transitional points • communication theory: levels, rules, congruence	• close tracking of self-reports about sequences of attempted solutions in context • definition of the "more of the same" sequences • determination of "who is the customer": the most motivated • understanding of the idiosyncratic language or world-view of the "customer"	• unit of therapy can be one person • therapist determines the "customer" goals and works to interdict the vicious cycles of mishandled attempted solutions through strategic directives (often symptom prescription)

Intergenerational themes are explored and utilized in the models of Bowen and Whitaker and, to a lesser extent, the Milan group. Minuchin, Haley, and the MRI group take an ahistoric approach to therapy. They prefer to track the current interactional sequences closely and to assume that history repeats itself in the form of these recurring transactional patterns.

Triadic processes are emphasized in the models of Bowen, Minuchin, Haley, and the Milan group.

A *normative family development* model is presented with increased clarity in the models of Whitaker, Haley, and Minuchin. These approaches underscore the importance of a model of normal family functioning in their therapy and diagnostic/assessment schemas. The Milan group, which has worked extensively with families of schizophrenic young adults, lacks the comparative range to build a model of normative family development. The MRI model, with its strict, problem-solving emphasis, does not utilize a model of normative family development. Bowen, like the MRI group, focuses mainly on a treatment unit of one (differentiation of self) but Bowen conceptualizes the problem in broader terms.

A similar dimension concerns each model's *theory of dysfunction* as it relates to the *family life cycle*. Several approaches—Haley, Minuchin, and MRI—explicitly discuss the likelihood of symptoms occurring at transition points in the family's life cycle. In relation to a theory of dysfunction, the Milan and MRI groups embody a *cybernetic epistemology*; the structural and strategic models, *an organizational epistemology*; and the Bowen theory and the symbolic-experiential approaches, an *intergenerational epistemology*.

All of the approaches share an appreciation for the need to understand the often implicit family rules as part of the diagnostic/assessment process. Similarly, the models uniformly link *rigidity* (of roles and patterns of interaction) to dysfunction. The *complementary, interdependent nature of symptoms* is particularly emphasized by Whitaker, Haley, Minuchin, and the MRI and Milan groups.

The role of the *extrafamilial, wider social contexts* in symptom production and maintenance has been a particular emphasis of the Milan group, Haley, and Minuchin. Their approaches stress the importance of including in the therapist's diagnosis/assessment the social contexts, such as referral source, hospital, and schools, which interact with the family.

The models of Bowen and the MRI group seem more adaptable to smaller *treatment* units (one person) than do the approaches of the Milan group, Whitaker (who prefers three generations in therapy), and Minuchin (whose enactment procedure for diagnosis and treatment demands more than one family member). Strategic therapy, as defined by Haley, is also adaptable to a small treatment unit, although larger ones are preferred.

On the issue of the *stance of the therapist* and the *therapeutic relationship*, there are some clear differences. The Bowen, Milan, and MRI models assume a more detached, less proximate therapeutic position than the other approaches do. Haley's strategic therapy falls somewhere between this extreme on the one hand and the highly proximate posture of the symbolic-experiential and structural models on the other. Bowen emphasizes remaining detriangled from the family emotional system, and the Milan team insists on the therapist's neutrality, while the MRI group conceive the therapeutic relationship more in terms of a consumer-oriented business transaction (with the customer and his or her language). Whitaker defines the therapeutic relationship as crucial to success and believes traditional diagnostic/assessment processes have the negative potential to interfere with this relationship. The structural model concurs with the importance of the therapeutic relationship. It defines joining, for example, as a mutual endeavor between therapist and family. For Whitaker, Minuchin, and Haley, diagnosis is more participatory, as the therapist is seen as a therapeutic instrument whose presence and interventions themselves yield the necessary assessment information.

On the variable of the *kind of assessment data* which the therapist is to seek, Bowen, Whitaker, and the Milan and MRI approaches all rely heavily on self-report data from family members. Haley and Minuchin tend to be more skeptical of the usefulness of this class of assessment information. They therefore organize sessions to produce in-session interactional data which serve as an isomorph to the interactions outside of therapy. From this viewpoint, problems—defined in structural and sequential ways—are most usefully and validly assessed when they are elicited in the very context that will seek to alter them.

The role of *feedback* from the family system has been discussed within the various perspectives. Bowen, the Milan and MRI groups, Minuchin, and Haley all agree on the importance of reading feedback after task assignment, and compliance or noncompliance. Whitaker, who does not utilize tasks/directives per se in therapy, agrees on the need to read feedback, especially as this relates to reading one's own emotional responses to the family.

The technique of *reframing* has been of particular importance to the strategic, symbolic-experiential, and Milan models, while for Minuchin, a similar concept would be *searching for strengths*. These operations have implications for the diagnostic/assessment process. They allow the therapist to not only perceive the dysfunctional aspects of a family's reality, but permit rapid and proactive movement toward changing these negative and pessimistic sides of family life.

CONCLUSION

This article has offered an exposition and comparative analysis of six major schools of family therapy. Understanding the diagnostic/assessment process for any model provides a useful isomorph for the remaining, interrelated aspects of the approach. The therapist's efforts in diagnosis/assessment serve as a guide to and preparation for the conduct of therapy. As expected, considerable consistency is found between the diagnostic/assessment schemas of the models and the corresponding interventions.

A number of issues relating to the diagnostic/assessment process have been raised in conducting the foregoing analysis. One matter is the degree to which family therapy models employ a fully developed model of normative family development in their diagnostic/assessment process. The link of the recent work on the family life cycle and normal family processes *and* the models' conception of normative family functioning is still weak. Two recent texts have contributed to the area of the family life cycle (Carter & McGoldrick, 1980) and normal family processes (Walsh, 1982), yet more work is needed by the proponents of the specific schools of thought.

In the past, the best formal work (e.g., generation of instrumentation) in family diagnosis/assessment has emerged more from family and marital researchers than from those proponents of a single school of therapy. The lack of clinical generalizability and utility of such findings has been a problem. The recent work of Reiss (1982), Beavers (1977), and Lewis, Beavers, Gossett, and Phillips (1976) is an exception, however.

Hoffman's recent book, *Foundations of Family Therapy,* offers a three-part critique of the recent research of David Reiss and his concept of the family paradigm. Her analysis of the value of Reiss' work can serve as a possible direction for the work of those interested in family diagnosis/ assessment. Hoffman writes:

> First, Reiss is continuing to examine family worlds in a truly systemic sense . . . Second, he is moving away from categorizing families on a scale from functional to dysfunctional, preferring to see dysfunction in relation to each family's idiosyncratic paradigm rather than to judge it in light of preconceived ideas of health and illness . . . Third, and perhaps most important, is Reiss' scrutiny of what happens when a family paradigm breaks down . . . A central issue for him is how family disorder and breakdown may create the opportunity for its own self-healing potential. (1981, p. 100)

Thus we can divine our guidelines for further development of family assessment/diagnosis schemas. First, they must be systemic, in the sense of taking into account relevant spheres of influence, and discussing and intervening into these spheres in a manageable and realistic way. Second, the degree to which a model-specific diagnosis/assessment schema can be useful in understanding the particular idiosyncrasies of the family in question must be considered. Finally, it has elsewhere been suggested that more intraschool specification of therapeutic methods will enable trainers to teach therapy more effectively (Liddle, 1982). Just so, more intramodel elaboration of what constitutes healthy family functioning *from that particular perspective* can provide more complex and useful therapeutic maps. In this manner, guidelines will be established that will not merely highlight dysfunction, but will proactively orient therapists to recognize and activate family resources and competencies.

REFERENCES

Beavers, W.R. *Psychotherapy and growth: A family systems perspective.* New York: Brunner Mazel, 1977.

Bowen, M. *Family therapy in clinical practice.* New York: Aronson, 1978.

Carter, B., & McGoldrick, M. *The family life cycle.* New York: Gardner, 1980.

Cromwell, R., Olson, D., & Fournier, D. Tools and techniques for diagnosis in marital and family therapy. *Family Process,* 1976, *15,* 1–50.

Fisher, L. Dimensions of family assessment: A critical review. *Journal of Marriage and Family Counseling,* 1976, *2,* 367–382.

Guerin, P., & Pendagast, E. Evaluation of family system and genogram. In P. Guerin (Ed.), *Family therapy: Theory and practice.* New York: Gardner, 1976.

Haley, J. *Problem-solving therapy.* San Francisco, Calif.: Jossey-Bass, 1976.

Hoffman, L. *Foundations of family therapy.* New York: Basic, 1981.

Keeney, B. Ecosystemic epistemology: An alternative paradigm for diagnosis. *Family Process,* 1979, *18,* 117–129.

Keith, D., & Whitaker, C. Symbolic-experiential family therapy. In A. Gurman & D. Kniskern (Eds.), *Handbook of family therapy.* New York: Brunner Mazel, 1981.

Kerr, M. Family systems theory and therapy. In A. Gurman & D. Kniskern (Eds.), *Handbook of family therapy.* New York: Brunner Mazel, 1981.

Lewis, J., Beavers, W.R., Gossett, J., & Phillips, V. *No single thread: Psychological health in family systems.* New York: Brunner Mazel, 1976.

Liddle, H.A. Family therapy training: Current issues, future trends. *International Journal of Family Therapy,* 1982, *4,* (2).

Minuchin, S. *Families and family therapy.* Cambridge, Mass.: Harvard, 1974.

Minuchin, S., & Fishman, C. *Family therapy techniques.* Cambridge, Mass.: Harvard, 1981.

Minuchin, S., Montalvo, B., Guerney, B., Rosman, B., & Schumer, F. *Families of the slums.* New York: Basic, 1969.

Minuchin, S., Rosman, B., & Baker, L. *Psychosomatic families.* Cambridge, Mass.: Harvard, 1978.

Napier, A., & Whitaker, C. *The family crucible.* New York: Harper & Row, 1978.

Neill, J., & Kniskern, D. *Selected writings of Carl Whitaker: The growth of a therapist.* New York: Guilford, 1982.

Reiss, D. *The family's construction of reality.* Cambridge, Mass.: Harvard, 1982.

Selvini Palazzoli, M., Cecchin, G., Prata, G., & Boscolo, L. *Paradox and counterparadox.* New York: Aronson, 1978. (a)

Selvini Palazzoli, M., Cecchin, G., Prata, G., & Boscolo, L. A ritualized prescription in family therapy: Odd days and evendays. *Journal of Marriage and Family Counseling,* 1978, *4,* 3–9. (b)

Selvini Palazzoli, M., Cecchin, G., Prata, G., & Boscolo, L. Hypothesizing, circularity, neutrality: Three guidelines for the conductor of the session. *Family Process,* 1980, *19,* 3–12. (a)

Selvini Palazzoli, M., Cecchin, G., Prata, G., & Boscolo, L. The problem of the referring person. *Journal of Marital and Family Therapy,* 1980, *6,* 3–9. (b)

Selvini Palazzoli, M., Cecchin, G., Prata, G., & Boscolo, L. Why a long interval between sessions. In M. Andolfi & I. Zwerling (Eds.), *Dimensions of family therapy.* New York: Guilford, 1980. (c)

Stanton, M.D., Todd, T., & Associates. *The family therapy of drug addiction.* New York· Guilford, 1982.

Walsh, F. (Ed.). *Normal family processes.* New York: Guilford, 1982.

Watzlawick, P., Jackson, D., & Beavin, J. *Pragmatics of human communication.* New York: Norton, 1967.

Watzlawick, P., & Weakland, J. *The interactional view.* New York: Norton, 1977.

Watzlawick, P., Weakland, J., & Fisch, R. *Change.* New York: Norton, 1974.

Weakland, J. Communication theory and clinical change. In P. Guerin (Ed.), *Family therapy: Theory and practice.* New York: Gardner, 1976.

Whitaker, C. The hindrance of theory in clinical works. In P. Guerin (Ed.), *Family therapy: Theory and practice.* New York: Gardner, 1976.

2. A Co-evolutionary Framework for Systemic Family Therapy

Lynn Hoffman, M.S.W.
The Ackerman Institute for
Family Therapy
New York, New York

Two

INTRODUCTION

THIS ARTICLE PRESENTS A METAPHORIC SCAFFOLD, A TIME Cable, from which to build an invisible building. The scaffold is temporary, to be torn down when the building is finished, but it can be recreated when a new building is contemplated. As with all such geospatial constructs, it is merely a diagram to hold in one's mind while mastering the systemic approach to family therapy pioneered by the Milan Associates, a group of four psychiatrists, Mara Selvini Palazzoli, Giuliana Prata, Gianfranco Cecchin, and Luigi Boscolo, who have been doing pioneering work in family therapy in Milan since 1967. Teachers of their model will find this diagram useful as a working tool.

The Time Cable addresses two aspects. One is vaguely temporal, having to do with differences in family patterns over time and how they relate to the presence of a symptom. The other is vaguely spatial, and represents what I and some of my colleagues (Peggy Penn, Jeffrey Ross, John Patten, Gillian Walker, and Joel Bergman) have called the "presenting edge"; that is, that salient bit of topology that seems most intensely to indicate: "Here is where we must direct our intervention." Since we always look at problems in context, it is not only the family context but that of other systems, including therapist or team, that gives us our presenting edge. Let me go on to a definition of terms.

SYSTEMIC FAMILY THERAPY

The term "systemic family therapy" (or just "systemic therapy," since the family unit is not always central) was adopted by the Milan Associates and has been formally used by them and others to describe their approach. In their introduction to *Paradox and Counterparadox* (1978a) they distinguish the premises underlying their hypotheses regarding "pathological" family systems from the premises underlying the physical sciences.

> The acceptance of these hypotheses requires an epistemological change, in the original sense of the Greek verb *epistamai*, which means to put oneself "over" or "higher" in order to better observe something. To do this, we must abandon the causal-mechanistic view of phenomena, which has dominated the sciences until recent times, and adopt a systemic orientation. With this new orientation, the therapist should be able to see the members of the family as elements in a circuit of interaction. None of the members of the circuit have unidirectional power over the whole, although the behavior of any one of the members of the family inevitably influences the behavior of the others. At the same time, it is epistemologically incorrect to consider the behavior of one individual the *cause* of the behavior of the others. This is because every member influences the others, but is in turn influenced by them. The individual acts upon the system, but is at the same time influenced by the communications he receives from it. (p. 5)

Although there has been some reluctance to use this term to describe the Milan Associates' approach, due to the fact that the word "systems" has been overused in the United States, I feel that it is an unfortunate necessity. It is important to have some name that will distinguish one model from another. The work of the Milan group has all too often been lumped with the approach of what has loosely been termed the "strategic" school. Although they acknowledge their debt to practitioners of this school, there are basic points of difference that are not always made clear. Their philosophy has been shaped with increasing care to reflect the thinking of Gregory Bateson.

For one thing, they have attempted to work in a noninstrumental manner. They do not, for instance, think of the therapist as a master strategist in a contest with the family. They also show a marked disinterest in terms like "resistance" or "control," although they have their own ways of dealing with these issues. In *Paradox and Counterparadox,* 1978a (much less so in *Self-Starvation,* 1978b) Selvini Palazzoli et al. do at times borrow from game theory and other adversarial analogies in describing families and family therapy, but these analogies do not seem to hold up if one watches the group at work.

For another thing, they are adamant about including the therapist and the referring context as part of the therapeutic unit. The therapist is never conceived to be "outside" or "above" the group or situation treated. The Milan team will often direct an intervention toward the therapist or the interface between the family and other professionals. This, for me, was a major shift in consciousness. I had paid lip service to the idea that I was included in my own treatment of a family, but had never subscribed to a therapeutic approach that brought that point home with such compelling clarity.

Co-evolution

Co-evolution was one of Bateson's (1979) primary illustrations for the workings of what he called "mental process" throughout the world of nature. Penn's fine paper "Circular Questioning" (1982), upon which much of this essay is based, describes the concept of co-evolution in far greater depth. It emphasizes the idea that just as a member of a species co-evolves together with a given environment, so does a repetitive behavioral sequence in a family—including a symptom—co-evolve together with a pattern of relationships. Bateson used what he called a "circular" or recursive model to explain the mutually reinforcing but constantly changing fit between the creature and its ecology. He felt this was a more appropriate model for explaining living systems than the simple linear causality of classical physics. Predictions are difficult to make if one abandons the linear view, because despite the enduring nature of some of the propositions that govern stability in living systems, there is always the chance event or random shuffle that may produce something new.

In conducting their interviews, the Milan group tracks the evolution of a symptom, as well as its present contextual fit. They then comment on this fit in such a way that the family is usually impelled to try to find a new evolutionary path. Many of their interventions can be seen as attempts to encourage the family to experiment with adaptive mutations that are within its repertory, but previously not permitted or perceived.

Keep in mind, however, that families are not species. The term co-evolutionary is merely an analogy that breaks down if it is applied too strictly. Furthermore, the Milan group does not use this term in talking about their work.

Time

Of all the dimensions addressed by the various schools of family therapy and their theories, the most loose and uncapturable is the concept of time. At one point, I joined those pioneers who rejected the importance of time to make a strong statement about their disagreement with psychodynamic theories of change.

Since the advent of the Milan Associates, my ideas have become considerably modified. Their interest in using historical data in the service of positively connoting behaviors in the present seemed to add a richness I felt was lacking in the horizontal, "here-and-now" views selected by structural and strategic lenses. However, the Milan uses of time are very different from the historical causality of Bowen (1978) or Boszormenyi-Nagy and Sparks (1973), which implies that understanding the precursors of behavior in the past will make it possible to change it in the present.

In general, the Milan Associates' use of time is relatively acausal. They will employ an apparently historical framework for their hypotheses or their positive connotation of family behaviors. But these hypotheses always point backwards and forwards at once and seem to collapse time into the kind of simultaneity represented by the story of the man who went to ask God for money.

> God, is it true that for you a thousand years are as a minute?
> Yes, my son.
> And God, is it true that for you a thousand dollars are as a penny?
> Yes, my son.
> Then, God, will you give me a penny?
> In a minute.

One gets the impression that there is no such thing as the simple present. It is always being influenced by expectations of the future, as inflation is said to be influenced by the expectations of the public. Equally, there is no such thing as the simple past. Everyone in the family has a different depiction of previous events, or different feelings about them. One goes on a search for something that is already ahead of one, just as one might look for a snake in the desert by the pattern it has left in the sand.

Even if time is an illusion, however, it is useful to keep the fiction that there is a past as well as a future, in order to highlight differences that can be used in the service of change. Let me describe my time diagram, to show how it works as a framework to hold in one's mind while interviewing a family.

The Time Cable

The Milan group, as I have said, creates a hypothesis that will explain the fit of the problem in a context that has co-evolved with the problem through time. They will use this impression of fit to positively reframe the problem as logical or even adaptive in the relationship system (or systems) in which it occurs. In their book *Change,* Watzlawick, Weakland, and Fisch (1974) speak of the "solution" to the problem becoming the problem. The Milan Associates add a new twist to this idea in their concept of positive connotation. The family's "solution" may not work precisely because, in some other sense, the problem is an even better "solution." It is a solution to a relationship dilemma the family seemingly cannot deal with any other way.

Penn, in her study of circular questioning, (1982) finds that the team tracks very closely not only relationship patterns in the present, but any shifts in allegiances at the time the problem first appeared. This discovery led me to revive a spatial model that had been suggested to me years ago by an advertising photograph of a coaxial cable. The cable speeds toward the viewer from some impenetrable mist of time, then is abruptly cut, so that a circular cross-section hits the viewer's eye.

In trying to think of a name for such a construct, I struggled with items that were long and round and could be cut, like frankfurters. These colorful images lost out to the more static but dignified term: Time Cable. I was trying to imagine a family as an endless river of interlocking strands, with separate strands or groupings representing persons or sub-groups. One could also envision larger cables encasing that one, and these would represent whatever other contexts are included, given the problem and its ecology. However multiple the nestings of cables or strands, any one of them could serve as contexts for any of the others.

Figure 2-1 The Time Cable

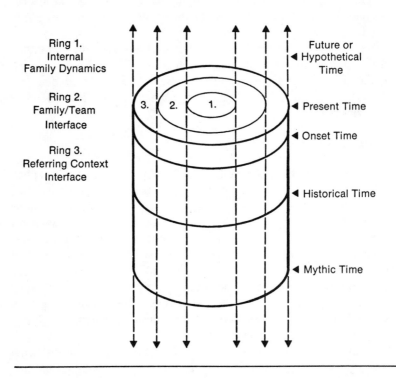

Figure 2-1 presents a diagram of this construct, sometimes still referred to by me as my Cosmic Sausage, because so much depends on where you cut it. In this case, we will assume that the cable's outer skin ends at the boundary of that imaginary entity called the family. The cuts in the cross-section correspond to different dimensions of time: present time, onset time, historical time, mythic time, and future or hypothetical time. At each position depicted by the Time Cable, "difference" questions work to clarify family alignments in relation to the problem, by revealing five aspects:

1. family alignments as they relate to the problem in the present
2. family alignments as they relate to onset
3. family alignments as they furnish a historical matrix for the problem

4. the effect on family alignments if the problem were to change
5. family alignments related to paradigmatic values that the problem metaphorically represents

Information thus gathered can be used both to build a hypothesis and to suggest a positive connotation of the problem in whatever temporal context seems most relevant.

The cable also contains subcylinders: Rings 1, 2, and 3 indicated within the cross-section in the present. The idea of the rings was to show that there are several systems interfaces one might have to consider in targeting an intervention, and there seemed to be an order of priority too. Interface dynamics within the family took second place to team/family dynamics, and both were usually outranked by the interface between the team/family system and professionals from the referring context. As I said before, the interface that seems most important in any interview can be called the "presenting edge." Having explained the design of the Time Cable, I will describe in detail how one uses these aspects of time in gathering information toward a hypothesis.

Differences Across and In Time

Milan-style "difference" questions, which form the core of their method of circular questioning, place under a microscope the connective tissue linking problems to family relationship patterns. Penn notes that a shift in such a pattern can coincide with that peculiar mutation known as a symptom (1982). We all know the folk saying, "It's an ill wind that blows nobody good." A daughter's drug-taking may coincide with the departure for college of mother's closest ally, a favorite oldest son. The girl's outrageous behavior keeps the mother from being overly preoccupied with the loss of the son and draws a previously distant father back into the picture, possibly into the first meaningful contact with mother in many years. Or, perhaps the son drops out of college and the drug-taking behavior subsides (or gets worse). Each element interacts recursively with and upon the others, with unpredictable results.

The Milan group's circular questioning technique warrants a brief digression in order to describe it. First, one must underline the importance the group accords to the ideas of Bateson, in particular the idea of "difference" (1979). For Bateson, information is news of a difference, and difference is a relationship or change in a relationship. With this in mind, the Milan Associates invented as a basic tool the triadic question:

"Gossip in the Presence of the Family" (Selvini Palazzoli et al., 1978a). This type of question involved asking one person about the relationship between two or more others. The therapist would then cross-reference the responses around the group. The content of these questions always involved differences: differences between perceptions of a dyad, primarily; but also differences in perceptions of other events. These difference questions could be divided into roughly three categories. One category would be more/less questions: Who, in response to Betty's sadness, is most worried? Or, on a scale of one to ten, who is closest to grandmother? Another category would be before/after questions: Was mother fighting with father more or less after grandfather moved away? A third category would be hypothetical questions, contrasting different present and future: "What is" with "What if?" If mother went out and got a job, what would be the effect on father? Johnny? Aunt May? These are all, of course, subdivisions of triadic questions. As they describe this process, the Milan Associates say,

> In this way, we can go beyond the triad and the sum of the various triads in the family. Thus the warp will pass through the woof until the design in the fabric will be clearly seen. (Selvini Palazzoli et al., 1980a)

Penn, who has analyzed a number of transcripts of the Milan Associates' sessions, uses a before–after arc to dramatize the difference between family coalitions at the onset of the problem and coalitions in the present. One might find in a set of questions about the problem the following kind of exchange:

Q: Who is most upset by the problem? A: Mother.
Q: What does mother do about it? A: She tries to motivate Johnny to go to school.
Q: Who agrees with mother about what she is doing? A: The school psychologist who is treating Johnny.
Q: Who disagrees? A: Father.
Q: Why? A: He thinks they are babying Johnny.
Q: Who feels the same as father? A: Grandmother.

Moving to onset time, one might find that the structure of relationships at this point changed drastically. The sequence might then go:

Q: When did the problem begin? A: A year ago.
Q: Was anything else happening a year ago? A: Grand-
father died.
Q: Who missed him most? A: Grandmother, then father.
Q: Who had the hardest time? A: Mother.
Q: Why? A: She and grandmother don't get along and
grandmother is now living in our house.

Thus one could see that Johnny's school refusal unites grandmother and father, who is her son, and gives grandmother and mother a way to express their distance. At the same time, the problem is pulling everyone together in the wake of an important death. A new balance is created (mother/psychologist vs. father/grandmother) with the boy mediating these two triangles. Based on this information, a comment might be made that positively reframes the problem as a solution to the family's new and precarious situation.

Yet other questions go back to the time when relationship patterns that seem to need protection first evolved. If two parents are made to believe by the therapist that the problem of their child is the glue that holds their marriage together, they may feel understandably defensive. But if one reaches back into the historical past one may find that there is no first mover. The parent–child triangle may have arisen to accommodate a previous triangle in which father could not break with his own family, because he was mediating between his father and his mother's mother. And so on, back. A positive connotation can be made, explaining the logic of the problem in the light of loyalties that were laid down in the distant past. As the notations accompanying the hexagrams in the Chinese *Book of Changes* or *I-Ching* put it: "No Blame."

An example of this kind of situation would be a young woman who, at age 26, went to Israel and there became converted to a cult group. The parents, not wishing to employ someone who would de-program her, and because she did not respond to individual therapy, brought her into family therapy. The parents came in alone the first session, because the daughter, suspicious of their motives, stayed away. The parents complained bitterly, the mother especially, about the behavior of this changeling child who had a teaching job but lived at home, trying to convert her parents and relatives to Christianity and leaving provocative literature around the house.

In the second session, attended by the girl and the oldest brother, a very different picture of the family problem emerged. The parents had for years fought bitterly over the husband's attachment to his own mother. This woman, now elderly, had never accepted her daughter-in-law or the family, referring to herself as mother-in-law even to her own son. She had lost a middle son exactly 26 years before, when the converted daughter was about to be born. The son was said to have committed suicide while he was mentally ill. The wife had named the daughter after him, as is common in a Jewish family, in the hope of recapturing the older woman's love. This attempt failed. Nevertheless, the husband persisted in trying to do everything he could for her and would visit her in a nearby nursing home at least once a week. The daughter complained that her parents would fight regularly about this visit, and that it was bad for her father, who had had two heart attacks. Since he was afraid to let himself get too excited he tended to bottle up his feelings. One reason the daughter stayed home was because she was the only person in the family he would express his feelings to.

When asked why they allowed the daughter to stay at home, despite the fact that the mother said that the situation was "eating out her insides," they said it was better than her living away. The mother said she had long noticed signs of emotional disturbance in her daughter, and felt her "symptoms" (God's voice telling her to leave Israel because she was needed to save her parents' marriage) were evidence that this incipient mental illness was now surfacing. Therefore she wanted to be able to watch over her. And the father admitted how much he would miss this girl, who was so close to him.

It seemed clear at this point that the conversion was a brilliant compromise. It brought the daughter back to mediate the marriage just as the youngest son left home; but at the same time broke the spell placed on her as the stand-in for the dead uncle. If she were no longer Jewish, she need not answer for the consequences of her name. And the mother declared that if her daughter married a Christian, she would turn away from her and treat her as if dead. So the implicit prophecy might be fulfilled, an eye for an eye, a child for a child, even while an actual death was not needed. This is just one example of a hypothesis containing a positive connotation on which any number of possible interventions could be built.

However, even this type of formulation may have a pejorative ring. One can then go back to family belief systems, represented by what I have called *mythic time*. Mythic time is at the bottom of the Cable, to signify that it comes from unknowable depths. Mythic time is expressed indirectly by family terms employed in describing the problem, or it is used to indicate some important attribute. "He takes *risks.*" (Who else in the family takes risks? Who is most worried about those who take risks?) "My mother was very artistic." (Who values artistic talent in the family most? Who else is artistic?)

Penn, using the phrase "cue words," acknowledges this aspect of the clinician's search (1982). What is indicated by these words or phrases is some strong value that is an organizer for experience in the family. Family legends or colorful ancestors add to this mythic dimension. Researcher David Reiss calls these "family paradigms," and says they act like a set of blueprints for processing new information that is handed down over generations (1980). At times, these lenses become outmoded. Reiss speculates that when paradigms shift, the greatest crises and symptomatic displays may ensue. Clinicians have often noted that symptomatic behavior seems to caricature some difference of style, belief, or opinion that could polarize or endanger family relationships. Such differences are usually not resolved but simmer endlessly, with the symptom often representing a metaphoric comment on the stalemate.

One could cite, for instance, the case of the child Elijah Wong, son of an elderly Chinese gentleman and a much younger orthodox Jewish woman, who was failing Hebrew school at the same time that in his spare time he was translating the story of Noah's Ark into Chinese.

Mythic time has a way of vanishing as soon as one thinks one has caught it, like water in the hand. It is betrayed by small clues, words, stories, analogic information, that is not usually part of a family's conscious knowledge about itself. Why, then, should a clinician strain to look for it? Because it gives information about feared disasters, often those very dangers that are evoked when one asks about the negative consequences of change, or the problems that would arise if the symptom went away. Being "liberated" in one family may be a prized value, but at either extreme catastrophe may lie. In one such family, when the family was asked what would happen if the presenting problem went away (an adolescent boy who kept running home from school and disrupting mother's new mid-life career), a sister "jokingly" said, "Father would have a heart attack." The other extreme, for a rebellious mother to give up her career, was equally frightening. The problem son confessed that the reason he came home from school was to see if his parents were divorced yet.

This kind of information provides a basis for a positive connotation, since it puts everyone in a good light and makes a villain out of no one.

To tell this boy to continue with his problem within the framework of the dilemma regarding liberation would be both nonblaming and unarguable.

The last dimension of Time Cable, future or hypothetical time, has been addressed by the Milan Associates in a most intriguing way. The idea of a different future always works to influence the present. The question of what might be some changes in the family if the problem were resolved not only taps into alternative universes of action but, in pointing to the range of probabilities, acts like a brake or a directional sign. If a fortune teller says, "I see an automobile accident within the next two weeks," this statement might make the hearer refrain from driving for a while or be particularly careful crossing streets. If she says, "I see a trip across water," the person may decide to take that European vacation after all, and who knows, meet the longed-for handsome stranger.

The Milan group can be chillingly direct in using hypothetical questions to make threats of action real in the present. They will ask, "If mother (who has a death phobia) did die, how would this affect the family?" Such questions put nightmare fears out on the table, blunting the possibility that they may come true. They are also used to validate hypotheses about negative consequences of change, asking about the disruptive effects should a problem disappear, and often uncovering an even more serious problem, thus validating an injunction to the problem person not to change, at least for the present. Notice the prevalence of phrases implying an escape hatch "for the time being," "until we can come up with a better solution." This also is a use of hypothetical time.

One is particularly struck by the use of the hypothetical, implying an alternate future, in the counterparadoxes devised by the Milan Associates. For instance: "When Mary reached adolescence, she saw that to grow up and leave the family in the normal way would be to leave mother alone with the task of caring for grandmother. Therefore, she decided to become ugly, stay at home, live like a nun, always there for grandmother, allowing mother to keep on working and having an active life." Or they might say that a son who has been lying in bed with the covers over his face knows that if he were to get up and find a job, his parents might miss their old job of worrying about him and begin to be bored with each other. Then they might divorce. Such messages tap into fears and possibilities which have been checked out during the session, but commenting on them in the intervention somehow makes the possibilities less real, assuming the interventions were on target. The girl in the first case might respond by finding a job or she might find a boyfriend (and mother might too). In the second case, the son might get up and go to work and the parents might indeed then start to find fault with each other. They might separate or they might not. Which action is taken in response to such messages is, of course, unpredictable.

The members of the Milan group state that they feel that circular questioning alone may bring about change. The constant evocation of different perceptions in a family about the same relationships or events, or differences in events over time, often leads family members (and the therapist) to a new place. This process gives no instructions, answers, or interpretations, consisting as it does of questions, but people quickly begin to put together a design for themselves under its aegis. I recall the case of one young man recovering from a psychotic episode who, after a particularly searching round of questions, said, "I think that when I was in the hospital, my parents got closer. Before, they were always quarreling. But when they came to the hospital, they would kiss each other, be nice to each other." A better positive connotation of his symptom could not possibly be described.

It is notable that members of a therapy team cannot usually keep themselves from adding a final message restraining the family from change, especially when there has been such an incontestable validation of their hypothesis. And perhaps it is precisely in the direction of less meddling and sparser interventions that this approach will begin to move, as its practitioners become more sophisticated.

Addressing the Presenting Edge

One of the most puzzling aspects of the Milan model is that the hypothesis about the development and continuation of a problem is central to the intervention, but the intervention may address very little of it. The two are not identical. Some interventions that positively connote and prescribe behaviors in the family may include a great deal of the hypothesis and some may not. Some interventions may address only the configuration in the present; others include information from the past.

Thus it is difficult to decide what goes into an intervention, and equally difficult to settle on a hypothesis. The family only gives up to the therapist a little part of its "truth" in any one session. And not only does this "truth" keep changing, but it is constantly being modified or even created by the encounter with the therapist. It takes hard work, observation, and intuition to get a "fix" on a family, a process that corresponds to locating a moving blip on a constantly changing time-space grid. The only way I know how to describe what I mean is to take the area of most tension and energy between therapist and family. It is like the carpenter tapping a wall to find the joist: where the hollow sound changes to a solid sound, it is there that he knows he can drive his nail. This place corresponds to the "presenting edge."

However, this image is far too instrumental to describe what I have in mind. It is too close to a description of what is popularly thought of as resistance. If one redefines resistance as an artifact of therapy, or a mote (sometimes beam) in the eye of the therapist rather than an attribute of the family, one gets a different view. Perhaps what we think of as resistance is only a signal from the host tissue that it wishes to continue with its present way of organizing itself and objects to the presence of a foreign body. Without the ability to detect what is and is not "itself," no living form would persist. So I often substitute the word "persistence" for resistance. Detecting the "presenting edge" means sensing where this persistence lies relative to the therapist's probe. Often this edge is not located in the family alone, but in an arc that includes family, therapist, and other professionals as well.

As a way of depicting this edge, I have resorted to another spatial metaphor: the Three Rings. These rings sit very nicely within the core of the Time Cable, since they represent some of the subcables that make it up. The center ring, Ring 1, consists of what is popularly known as "family dynamics." This ring may represent interlocking strands that go back three or more generations and include collateral families as well. I imagine that the wires making up the various strands are like individuals in the families or kin group. The relationship between those strands at any given time, rather than the history of a single thread, is the proper concern for family therapy.

The second ring represents a recursive loop comprising the relationship between therapist or team and family. This loop includes all issues pertaining to the therapy/family interface: membership, spacing of sessions, induction of the therapist into the family system, and matters like that.

Ring 3 corresponds to what the Milan Associates have called "the referring context" (Selvini Palazzoli, 1980). It includes other professionals, agencies, and institutions that may be involved in the case, or even the work context of family therapist or team.

In deciding which edge to address in any intervention, first priority is given to the system that seems most likely to undermine the therapy process, and that one is often the referring context. One is reminded of that elegantly circular children's game: stone, scissors, paper. Just as stone can vanquish scissors, so people from the professional context can knock out or negate the efforts of the family therapist or team. If this is happening, the professional edge must be deferred to or prescribed.

Ring 2, the family/team interface, comes next in importance, as a general rule, and corresponds to what Carl Whitaker, using a power metaphor, has called the administrative battle (1969). If being in charge of treatment issues is problematic, then this is the edge that must be addressed. Sometimes the family has to be given up or may drop out, but that is better than continuing with a futile effort to deal with a family that can appear or disappear like the genie in Aladdin's lamp.

The interior ring, representing family issues, usually takes last place to the other two. Only when interface politics at the edges of Rings 3 and 2 are settled can one get to what is going on in the family itself. Even here one must be wary. If two parents come in, one declaring that Johnny's disinterest in school is a problem and the other declaring that it is perfectly healthy and good, this is not a Ring 1 issue. It is a disagreement about coming into treatment. It belongs to the therapist/family edge, and even though one can use information about the way other conflicts in the family are tied to this edge when one makes an intervention, the intervention may well warn against the dangers of treatment. It might cite the disagreement between the parents over the problem as protective of the family, since coming in to treatment might bring up issues that would be painful, disruptive, or both.

Interventions that address the central ring are naturally based on richer and more complex information, since one is dealing with an entity with a past and a future. But it may be that the therapist or team must leave this edge from time to time. Just as paper can envelop stone, so a family may draw in an outside professional whenever intolerable changes loom. In this way, therapy may be seen to be as recursive a process as the above-mentioned children's game.

This concept is dramatically new for many family therapists, whose more linear epistemology has allowed them to experience themselves as "change agents" acting upon the family, the "subject," in a unidirectional fashion. The belief that understanding and working with family dynamics comprised the whole therapeutic undertaking was characteristic of the first generation of family therapists. For those who, like me, came of age during that generation, it was a revelation to realize that one is part of a larger circuitry *always,* even when the outer contexts are not operative.

The following clinical examples are taken from observation of the Milan Associates in Italy in 1978-1979, when all four members of the team were still together. They have graciously allowed me to draw on the notes I made while watching the sessions from behind a screen.

Case Example #1

In the following case, only the center ring was addressed, since the referring context was checked out and the family offered no blocks to treatment. The therapists were Giuliana Prata in the room and Mara Selvini behind the screen. The family consisted of mother, father, and a 6-year-old boy. They had been referred by another family therapist who had failed to make any headway during several months of treatment.

The problem was little Alessandro, who had been diagnosed as psychotic. He was constantly running around the room or hitting his mother. He also refused to speak, except to say Yes or No. His irrational behavior started the previous Christmas, when he insisted on sleeping in his parents' bed. He had started nursery school that fall, but his behavior caused him to be dropped from school. His mother was not working, although she had held a job until the boy was three, leaving him with her husband's mother. Since then she had chosen not to work.

Four questions were singled out to ask during the pre-session:

1. What was the current involvement of the referral person?
2. Why was Alessandro placed with his paternal rather than his maternal grandmother?
3. Why did the wife stop working when Alessandro was three?
4. What happened the previous Christmas when Alessandro's symptoms started?

The answers were: first, the referring doctor was no longer in the picture. Second, Alessandro stayed with the father's mother because his family was better off. Third, the wife stopped working because the husband got sick, but after he recovered she did not go back even though she wanted to because he opposed her doing so.

The fourth question was the most interesting. When Prata asked how they had spent Christmas Day, the parents said they had spent it alone. I was sitting behind the screen watching Selvini. She seemed to swell up to a larger size and became very excited. She was in the process of what I call "smelling the rotten meat." She kept muttering, "Impossible! Impossible! A couple in Italy not to spend Christmas with the relatives? Impossible!" She called Prata out and had her question the parents more closely about what had happened at that time. It seemed that Selvini was right on target. The father, on Christmas Eve, had quarreled very badly with the maternal grandmother over a present she had brought for Alessandro. Even though he later apologized to his mother-in-law, the mother was very upset. That night Alessandro got into bed between his parents. Since then, he came into bed with them every night and sex had become impossible.

But there had been other changes. Previously, the husband used to get angry with his wife and make scenes, after which he would go to visit his mother. Since Alessandro's irrational behavior began, he no longer made scenes. At that time they had been living farther from the husband's mother than the wife's mother. Recently, they had moved closer to the husband's mother. At this point in the conversation, Alessandro began to run about the room. Prata stopped him, drawing him to her and congratulating him for knowing how to keep the peace between his parents. She said, "You went to your parents' bed on Christmas because your father was angry with your grandmother and that way your mother didn't have to make love with father." The little boy smiled knowingly, nodded his head and said "Si." Prata then found out that the wife was now more unhappy than the husband; she still wished to work and her husband did not want her to. However, Alessandro was such a problem that he took up all her time.

The final message, delivered by Prata, went as follows: "There is indeed indication for family therapy. But you, Alessandro, are doing something very useful for your father and mother. You are doing two positive things, one for father and one for mother. By acting crazy, you stopped father from having scenes so mother could get some rest. By acting crazy, you also keep mother from going to work, and so father is happy because he likes her to stay at home. Will you promise to go on being crazy until the next meeting?" Alessandro again nodded his head and said, "Si."

If one analyzes this intervention and the positive reframing of the child's getting into bed between the parents delivered during the session, one sees that these two messages deal with a shift in the family. Mother had moved to an inferior position in relation to father. As long as she worked, she was happy. Also, even though Alessandro was being cared for by the father's mother, they were living closer to her mother. There was a balance of sorts which seemed to persist even after the mother stopped working. Then came a period when Alessandro went to nursery school and this brought up the possibility of the mother working again. The couple also moved closer to the father's mother. The father now seemed to be "ahead" on the subject of work, and also on the question of which mother to live closer to. The mother seemed quite depressed. The father's fight with the maternal grandmother on Christmas Eve may have been a reaction to the tighter coalition between the mother and her own mother. This then may have triggered the irrational behavior of Alessandro; who in fact not only resolved the issue of the mother working but prevented wifely retaliation in bed by eliminating sex entirely. The boy's problem, mimicking the positions of both mother and father, took on both sides of the quarrel. So effective was this behavior in masking the quarrel that the previous therapist had no inkling of it. In a fine illustration of circular reactions, the child's craziness blocked the possibility of open friction, just as the possibility of open friction heightened the craziness of the child.

Case Example #2

The next example is a two-part sequence. The first session deals with the family's stated indecision regarding family treatment, and so represents Ring 2. The patient was a 17-year-old boy, Carlo, who six months before started to wash his hands and his genitals so frequently that he could no longer go to school. He had a younger brother of 15. The father held a position in the business of his own younger brother, the "rich Uncle Paulo." Several years before, the brother had divorced his wife. His wife and son had then moved away. At this time the father, against the advice of his mother, went to work for his brother.

The relationship between the mother and father was the one of domineering husband and subservient wife. The father was extremely close to his mother, and the wife stated how jealous and excluded this relationship made her feel. However, it seemed as if the wife took some importance from the position she had with the rich uncle. When her husband had first gone into the business, the two families had become very close; in effect, the younger brother had "borrowed" the older brother's family. Carlo was a particular favorite, both of the uncle and of the father's mother. Based on this information, the team made something like the following interpretation:

> Carlo is the true repository of the love of grandmother and uncle. At a certain point, he felt that if he developed too fast, he would surpass his father and brother. Therefore, out of loyalty to them, he sacrificed his growth and independence.

The doubts we have about accepting this case are that if the family comes into therapy, Carlo will surpass his father and his brother and there will be even bigger problems.

The parents were shocked by this statement; the father saying that he was worried that Carlo would take advantage of it to become worse, and the mother saying, with admirable tactfulness, "This is an unexpected but clarifying conclusion." The family reported in the second session that Carlo's symptoms had cleared up for the next three weeks, and had only returned the week before the next session. In addition, he had become very cold and distant with his mother and much friendlier with his brother, going out with him instead of staying in his room as he had done before.

The interpretation seemed correct, in view of the impact on the problem, but it was unclear why, in this family situation, the symptom appeared when it did and so suddenly. One clue was that the mother, described by the father as having been depressed for many years, stopped being depressed when Carlo's problem started. Another clue was that the onset of the symptom coincided with a change in the family: the rich uncle's son, now grown to manhood, had been given an important position in the firm. It turned out, too, that the rich uncle had remarried. The mother and Carlo had to some extent lost their favored positions with him, even though the mother said that the only reason she cared about their position with this uncle was because they depended financially on him.

It still seemed mysterious why the boy should begin to have his problem at the moment his cousin came into the firm. Then the mother gave the hint that led to a possible solution. Carlo was much loved by the new wife, and he also got along quite well with the cousin. The mother declared her plan of having Carlo spend the impending summer vacation with the rich uncle's family. It was possible that she hoped that Carlo would win the love of the uncle back to them. During the whole session, she sat very close to Carlo, constantly stroking him and leaning next to him, which he passively allowed.

The "lineage" of the problem now began to seem clear: the wife, treated as an inferior by her husband, placed great store by her connection with the rich uncle, who was so much more powerful than her husband. When the husband allowed himself to be persuaded to join his brother's business, against his mother's wishes, the wife "won" a better position for herself, and won a point against the rival mother-in-law. With the advent of the uncle's new wife, her only entrance ticket was the love the uncle had for Carlo. But when he, too, was supplanted by the uncle's son, the mother must have felt totally defeated. At this point, she must have placed pressure on Carlo to make himself liked by the incoming cousin, and to be especially charming to the uncle's new wife. Carlo was thus caught in a game which seemed to embody a struggle between the husband and wife, although it involved the mother-in-law and the rich uncle and other family members. The impending catastrophe was that since the rich uncle had reconstituted his own family, so to speak, he would no longer need his brother's family.

An earlier version of Carlo's position was suggested by a story the mother told about Carlo when, at the age of six, he would visit the father's mother. Father claimed that his mother loved Carlo very much and that the boy loved her. His wife contradicted him, saying that Carlo would cry for her whenever he had to visit grandmother. Hearing this dispute, Carlo disqualified his part in the entire transaction by saying, "I only cried because I was sick." The best way to disqualify himself from taking any position in the family wars, which were intensifying at present, would be to once more develop a symptom and be "sick."

This hypothesis was based on a more thorough analysis of the family situation than had previously been possible. The intervention chosen was a ritual given to all members of the family. It consisted of a letter that each person was to read to Carlo at the end of the session. The messages tied together all the threads of the hypothesis, not only linking the three generations, but also the two collateral families, in a complex web in which all parties were cross-referenced. Instructions were given to read the letters again, in the same way, at the hour once a month during the vacation when the session would have been held:

Father's letter
Dear Carlo: Thank you for having decided to fail in school and have symptoms because in this way Uncle Paulo's family will never have the courage to abandon us and this will prevent your mother from once more having a severe depression.
Your Papa.

Mother's letter
Dear Carlo: Thank you for having decided to fail in school and have symptoms because in this way Uncle Paulo's family will never have the courage to abandon us and this will

prevent your father from repenting the fact that he disobeyed his Mama.
       Your Mama.

Brother's letter
Dear Carlo: Thank you for having decided to fail in school and have symptoms because if you do all this work for our family, I will be free to do what I want.
       Your Brother.

The father and brother were able to read their letters to Carlo but the mother broke down weeping and was hardly able to read hers to the end. The family left in stunned silence. Although this writer does not know what the outcome was, this is a good example of a ritual in which the family members, at the behest of the team, positively connoted the son's behaviors, and in the case of husband and wife, touched upon deeper issues.

My last example, a consultation, addresses a struggle between the judiciary system and the family system with the therapist unhappily caught in the middle. Here the history of the problem was obtained during the presession, but was not central to the team's intervention.

Case Example #3

This was a pair of young, Central American parents who had emigrated to North America to make their fortunes. They had left their 2-year-old daughter, Tania, with the husband's parents who were Hindu. Since the wife's parents were Black and came from a lower socioeconomic class, the husband's parents had looked down on the marriage from the beginning. When Tania was 5, the mother prevailed upon the father to bring her to live with them, as she felt the in-laws were poisoning Tania's mind against her. In the meantime, another girl, Maya, was born. When Tania arrived, the mother found her hostile and disobedient, and beat her severely enough to bring in the authorities. The court took both the older child, now 7, and the younger, who was refusing to eat and was not thriving, and placed them in a foster home. The court then remanded them back to the parents' care, on condition that the family enter family therapy. Whether the children would stay in the home or go back into foster care depended on the opinion of the therapist who was treating them. A social worker from the foster home was still involved with the mother. The therapist, a Black psychologist, also learned that the parents believed in black magic, or "Obeah." They felt that it was being used against their family, and the father had gone to see a spiritualist priest. The therapist felt he was losing what little leverage he had with the family and asked the Milan team for help.

The team asked him to interview the family while they watched from behind a screen. The therapist asked how the children were doing, and the mother said that Tania now felt she could get away with any kind of disobedient behavior, and that Maya was still not eating properly. Both parents looked defeated and depressed.

The team then called the therapist out. They told him to ask the family two questions: First: "What percent influence do you think Obeah has on the family; Second: "What percent influence does the family therapy have?" To the first question the parents answered 90 percent. To the second, the father said that at first family therapy had more influence but now he would put it at 20 percent, and the mother agreed. Because of the power of Obeah, the father said, "nothing we do is right."

The team then asked the therapist to go out and have coffee with the family. After they had composed their message, they reconvened the family and the therapist. The message, spoken by Selvini, went as follows:

> We have seen that you are a very united family with strong bonds. Your family does not need family therapy at all. Every family has problems, but you do not need family therapy. What we see is that you have had many negative influences on your family—your relatives, the court, have all worked against your unity. Unfortunately, the court and the Children's Aid Society have ordered you to go to therapy. You must be patient and come to meetings until the court is convinced that everything is all right. Poor Dr. Jonas has a problem too. He is working under a force stronger than he is, just as you are—so you're in the same boat. But be patient—perhaps you can come to a unity after all.

The effect on the parents was dramatic. They were surprised, pleased, and relieved. But the effect on the therapist was even more dramatic. He told the team that they had helped him out of a situation where he felt totally ineffective. The parents were only coming in because they were forced to by the court. "This prescription took me out of the coalition with the enemies," he said. He also said that while having coffee with the family, the father mentioned that the priest had told him that intruders were using Obeah to break up his family. The team's message thus lined up very well with the priest's message.

This consultation interview is typical of what the Milan Associates call "impasse therapy." The intervention will be targeted at the edge where the therapist is stuck with the family. Here the initial problems originating in the struggle between the mother and the father's parents, with the child caught between them, had evolved into a matching struggle between the family and the juvenile court system with a therapist caught between them. The intervention implied that the relatives, backed by Obeah, and the court, were the intruders trying to break up the family, and joined the therapist and the family in a benevolent coalition against them.

As the reader can see, these interventions are both simple and complex. They may be directed primarily at an edge external to the family itself, but they do include references to important intrafamily issues. In addition, present, onset, historical, future, and mythic aspects of time are variously interwoven together in these interventions, as dictated by the hypothesis and the sense of what edge was salient in each situation. In the first case, the presenting edge was clearly family dynamics. An onset question was used to reframe the child's sleeping in the parents' bed, but the final intervention was directed at his behaviors in the present. In the second, the first intervention was directed primarily at the team/family interface. This intervention, by tying problems in the family to a perceived danger in the family coming into treatment, made hypothetical time paramount.

In the second intervention, the young man's symptom was prescribed in a ritual that cross-referenced elements of the struggle between the parents that touched three generations. Historical factors as they influenced family dynamics in the present became the "presenting edge." In the third example, the referring context was the presenting edge, but the family situation was addressed and all the "forces" working against its unity were placed together. These included the power of Obeah, and mythic time was brought into this intervention as well. One cannot make a cookbook for this approach to therapy; but the room for variety and ingenuity, and the refreshingly idiosyncratic nature of each intervention, as it tailors itself to the idiosyncratic nature of each therapeutic situation, is impressive.

CONCLUSION

If, in responding to a family in trouble, we can capture and play back our sense of the workings of the process whereby a particular symptom co-evolves within a particular family group, we will have respected that which Bateson called "embodiments of mind" in living systems (1979). The Time Cable is one framework among many for seeing how "mental process" in each family operates. If the therapist shares this understanding with a family, and changes course continually as the family responds to what the therapist shares, the therapist becomes part of the family in a noninstrumental and truly recursive way.

However, it is important to be part of, not swallowed up by, the family. To do this, one must keep one foot always outside the family system; hence the importance of the team, or peer supervisory group, or even adding an observation group to the team, as Luigi Boscolo and Gianfranco Cecchin now do in teaching their method. Being thus simultaneously in and out of the system is of the essence and yet hard to achieve. One is reminded of a passage by Henri Michaux, a Belgian poet, who comments on his experiences in *The Country of the Magicians* (1977).

> To walk on both sides of a river at once is an exhausting experience.
> One often sees a student of Magic go up a river by walking on both banks simultaneously. He is so absorbed he doesn't notice you, because this feat is extremely difficult and requires complete concentration. If anything were to distract him, he might end up by walking on only one bank. What an unbearable humiliation that would be!

In this image, the river corresponds to the Time Cable, and the student, the river, and the two opposing banks represent the systems and the interfaces between systems that must be considered in teaching this complex therapeutic approach.

REFERENCES

Bateson, G. *Mind and nature.* New York: Dutton, 1979.
Boszormenyi-Nagy, I., & Sparks, G. *Invisible loyalties.* New York: Harper & Row, 1973.
Bowen, M. *Family therapy in clinical practice.* New York: Aronson, 1978.
Michaux, H. *The country of the magicians.* Atlantic Highlands, N.J.: Humanities, 1977.
Penn, P. Circular questioning. *Family Process,* 1982, *21.*
Reiss, D. The working family: A researcher's view of health in the household. Distinguished Psychiatrist Lecture, Annual Meeting, American Psychiatric Association, San Francisco, Calif., 1980.

Selvini Palazzoli, M. The problem of the referring person. *American Journal of Marital and Family Therapy*, 1980, *2*, 3-9.

Selvini Palazzoli, M., Cecchin, G., Boscolo, L., & Prata, G. *Paradox and counterparadox.* New York: Aronson, 1978. (a)

Selvini Palazzoli, M., Cecchin, G., Boscolo, L., & Prata, G. *Self-Starvation.* New York: Aronson, 1978. (b)

Selvini Palazzoli, M., Cecchin, G., Boscolo, L., & Prata, G. Hypothesizing, circularity, neutrality. *Family Process*, 1980, *19*, 3-12.

Watzlawick, P., Weakland, J., & Fisch, R. *Change: Principles of problem formation and problem resolution.* New York: Norton, 1974.

Whitaker, C. The growing edge. In J. Haley & L. Hoffman (Eds.), *Techniques of family therapy.* New York: Basic, 1969.

3. Reflections on Assessment in Structural Family Therapy *

---

*This article was originally presented in part at the Harvard Medical School conference, Family Therapy, April 26 and 27, 1982.

H. Charles Fishman, M.D.
Director
Family Therapy Training Center
Philadelphia Child Guidance Clinic
Assistant Clinical Professor of Psychiatry
University of Pennsylvania
Philadelphia, Pennsylvania

The author gratefully acknowledges suggestions for this article from Bradford Keeney, Ph.D., Braulio Montalvo, M.A., and Bernice Rosman, Ph.D.

Three

"I am a verb."
> Gregory Bateson

"Happy families are all alike; every unhappy family is unhappy in its own way."
> Leo Tolstoy

IN SPITE OF THE CONTEMPORARY HABIT OF VIEWING FAMILIES in process and as evolving social organisms, every clinician works from some conceptual notion of a family's dysfunction and addresses treatment accordingly. Yet it is the rare family therapist who speaks comfortably of *diagnosis*; a word that conjures images of the medical model, which, at the very least, tends to be constraining and pathologizing. Such a model is widely held by family therapists to be counterproductive for the systems clinician who is working toward change rather than "cure."

The two quotes at the beginning of this article, one by Bateson and one by Tolstoy, typify the dilemma faced by the family therapist. On the one hand, we vigorously espouse the notion that people are verbs, constantly in flux, part of an evolving process. This partition is typified by the words of Hegel, "The true is thus the bacchanalian whirl in which no member is not drunken; and because each, as soon as it detaches itself, dissolves immediately—the whirl is just as much transparent and simple repose" (Kaufmann, 1965). Conceptualizing people as verbs, the therapist gives importance not to illusions of stability and static existence, but instead to the ever moving, dynamic, and ephemeral aspects of families that allow for the expansion of self and the family's continuous movement toward increasing complexity.

On the other horn of the dilemma is the notion espoused by Tolstoy: that there are regular patterns. I submit, however, that the Tolstoy quote has it backwards. The unhappy families that we clinicians work with tend to be stereotyped, repetitive, and redundant, while the happy families have variety and flexibility, and often invent innovative solutions to common problems of living. Hence, unhappy families are alike; happy families differ.

The notion that families are stable patterns of organization rests on the observation that a system has rules that dictate regular relationships between its members. These patterned relationships are responsible for the social definition of a person, since, in a contextual sense, the individual entails the person plus his or her salient social context.

The dilemma posed by defining the family as a noun or as a verb has important implications for the clinician. If the clinician focuses on the patterns, he or she risks reifying dysfunctional structure. Conversely, if he or she focuses only on the family in flux, then where does the clinician direct therapy? Certainly not at the symptom, a chimerical beast with an embarrassing penchant for spontaneous improvement, even on waiting lists.

Assessment in structural family therapy has, as an integral part of its technique, a resolution of this dilemma. In this article I shall discuss this question, as well as how the structural therapist assesses families.

Case Example

The Williams family, consisting of two parents and four children, ages 15, 13, 10, 7, presented itself because the oldest, Bill, Jr., was failing at his high school for the academically talented. The parents, in their early thirties, had separated for six months during the previous year, but had reunited a few months prior to treatment. Father is employed as a janitor while mother is a full-time nursing student who works evenings as a salesclerk.

Every system except the universe is a subsystem and, as such, is arbitrarily delineated. Therefore, to facilitate assessment, we can look at two separate systems: the family, and the family plus therapist.

This article is divided into three parts: the first dealing with assessment by the observer outside the family system; the second with the observer as part of the system; and the third, in which the observer, via the technique of enactment, is simultaneously both inside and outside of the family.

THE OBSERVER OUTSIDE OF THE SYSTEM

Assessment in structural family therapy is based on two traditions. The first, "Occam's razor," holds that the simplest explanation is best. Therefore, in searching for a way of conceptualizing families, the structural family therapist tries to use the simplest parameters. The second tradition on which assessment is based is the value of open observation of phenomena. If a phenomenon cannot be directly observed and described, then it is considered less valid than one that can. The closer one stays to observable data, in contrast to abstract theorizing, the better.

What these ideas mean operationally can be demonstrated in the context of the Williams family. First, even though structural family therapy advocates the necessity for direct observation, the therapist, nevertheless, forms certain hypotheses about the family on the basis of intake data prior to the first meeting. On the basis of this data, the therapist formulates the following hypothesis:

Case Example
I assume this family, like any family that presents, is in "crisis." This means that the rules that previously worked are no longer operating satisfactorily. The symptom emerged to stabilize the system, albeit at an earlier developmental organization and at a cost to the growth of the individuals and family. What might have thrown this family into crisis? Three of the children are now in, or just entering, puberty, which exerts great pressure on the family to change. The couple is in their mid-thirties, and in blue collar families, the "40-year-old life crisis" of white collar workers tends to occur ten years earlier. Mother returned to school; a move probably also prompted by the pressures of the larger culture; both financial and social, namely, the women's movement, as well as by the developmental pressures within the family.

The intake sheet also describes the family's problem, typed verbatim in the caller's words. In this case, father walked into the clinic and reported the following problem: "Billy is 16 and has been doing poorly in school for the last year. He is flunking three subjects. But he has been a problem since day one." The intake worker also writes, "Father could not give children's dates of birth or ages. So I had his wife call to complete application." Mother called and said, "Billy goes from being very unhappy to being in a depression. He has a hard time expressing himself."

From this kind of information, the therapist generates hypothetical structure. Father, whose language is more behaviorally oriented, is more distant than mother, who is concerned with Billy's feelings. It sounds like Billy has been the identified patient for his entire life and has been functioning to help stabilize the homeostasis by misbehaving. "His" problems may have exacerbated at this point since mother and father have been having more problems while, of course, they may have been more troubled, since Billy, an adolescent, has been increasingly away from the house. A fascinating part of this intake is the way the intake worker was inducted into reinforcing both father's peripherality (he did not know the children's dates of birth, or even ages) and mother's centrality. Rather than asking that father find the necessary data and call back, the worker had mother call to finish the application.

The therapist then meets the family. Father is a quiet spoken, average looking man, wearing a blue shirt and work pants. Mother, a strikingly pretty woman, is dressed like a hip college student. The younger children are dressed in the uniform of the Catholic school.

The family enters the room. Mother and Billy sit together with the other children clustered on the other side of the woman. Father, also in the circle, sits slightly out, his legs crossed away from his wife. Penny, the youngest and the only girl, oscillates between father's and mother's laps.

Father starts talking, haranguing Billy for failing in school. Mother shifts towards the boy. They both fold their arms across their chests. As Billy argues, mother at first says nothing. Then she enters, parroting her husband's words but in a tone that is soft and loving. Meanwhile, she does not look in her spouse's direction, even when he addresses her.

The structural therapist takes this data to further strengthen his initial hypothesis. The process suggests that it is not father but mother who is enmeshed with Billy. Father is "odd man out," with mother and the children overly close.

The therapist can thus perceive patterns and describe them. But, in so doing, does he or she distort the process and hence impede treatment? Are we opting for the categorization implied by Tolstoy's quote and vilified by systemic therapists?

Of course, one cannot escape some regularity and pattern in natural systems. Ashby, in *An Introduction to Cybernetics* (1956), as well as

Design for a Brain (1952), describes how behavior tends to converge. At the initiation of a social system, transactions may appear random, but soon the behavior converges, and becomes rule-governed. Anyone who has ever gone to a party with strangers knows how rapidly rules become established between people, and how difficult these rules are to break.

One way out of this dilemma is to state that we are not observing a static entity as we would a rock formation, but we are evaluating the family as it changes over short periods of time, instead. Hence, we are less liable to fix, or "pickle" the family like a biological specimen. Unfortunately, this reasoning is begging the question. True, the rule-bound, "converged" behavior which appears to the clinician as patterns is based on movement, that is, it is predicated on the interactions between family members. But, as Shands (1971) points out, movement is the sine qua non, the irreducible condition for the most basic types of knowing. In seeing, for example, the eye has to move continuously; in touching or feeling, if the palpating motion is not continued "adaptation soon takes place and the tactile data fade out of central attention to be quickly brought back into the attention again by unexpected movement" (Shands, 1971, p. 26). Thus movement, whether it occurs in the eye of the observer only, or in both the observer and in what is observed, is basic to knowing. This concept will not resolve the Bateson/Tolstoy dilemma, but it does help to elucidate the assessment process in structural therapy.

According to Shands, movement that is observed, however, soon is discovered to have another basic characteristic, namely that it is regular and repetitive. As one continues to watch, one finds that the observables begin to be organizable in one or more ways. One begins to know where and how to observe. One learns what to expect. The notion of the repetitive or regular can further be translated into the notion of patterns (Shands, 1971).

The clinician then watches the family in "motion" as interactions transpire, and he or she scans to ascertain patterns. First, in Bateson's terms, the therapist looks for "information, meaning a difference that makes a difference" (Bateson, 1979) in the ways in which family members relate. Who reacts when Billy states that he doesn't do his homework because his father's heavy drinking and the ensuing parental fight upset him? The structural therapist tracks closely to ascertain how mother reacts to her son's attack on her husband. Mother sits, staring at her son and then at her husband, without helping her husband in his attempt to separate the two issues. Then, supporting the boy and vitiating father's initiative, the woman says, "Billy, I know you try hard."

These transactions convey information to the therapist. Mother is closer, more protective and emphathetic in her relationship with Billy than is father. Father is less emphathetic and more task oriented in his dealings with his son than is his wife and thus can be described as more distant. Billy's greater closeness to mother is manifested by his being warmer and more attentive to her than he is to his father.

The structural therapist organizes these observations into patterns. But we can address ourselves to two kinds of patterns. There are those patterns that help govern the family's behavior as a subsystem in relation to *outside* subsystems. Then, there are those patterns that involve the behavior of the individual subsystems *within* the family. Perhaps if we direct our therapeutic efforts toward the family as an entire unit and not the specific parts individually, then we will be able to better resist having our evaluation stabilize the dysfunctional family further.

The work of Maturana (1978) and Varela (1979) is useful in distinguishing these two types of patterns, a distinction that they call organization and structure. Using these terms more generally than Maturana and Varela do, we can say that organization refers to the rules that maintain its wholeness. Organization is ascertained as the family as a whole interacts with other subsystems. Structure, on the other hand, refers to the relationships between the components within the system, the internal workings. Structure is ascertained, in part, by intervening differentially with the different components. Supporting one spouse and seeing how the system responds is an example.

Much systemic therapy is geared toward intervening in this way. The most topical example of this is Mara Selvini Palazzoli and Giuliana Prata's "invariable prescription," (1982) in which they utilize the same therapeutic directive for schizophrenic and autistic families regardless of the specific relationships between the family members. They deal with the family in its entirety, en masse, rather than with the structural components.

But this approach again rigidifies. True, it does not risk reifying the internal family structure since it deals only with the organization. This therapy leads toward reification between the therapist and the family, since the same "prescription" creates out of diverse families the same configuration. The immovable therapists clash with the family, obliging the family, regardless of its shape initially, to fit into the "invariable" mold. Thus, rather than construe a pattern in the family and reify it, this approach reifies by imposing the same pattern.

Structural therapy, in contrast to the approach of Mara Selvini Palazzoli, emphasizes the actual relationships between the parts. As such, it is a therapy of subsystems—the spouse, parent, sibling, individual, and family subsystems—as well as special interest groupings. The structural therapist uses proximity and distance between subsystems as parameters to evaluate families. Who is close, overly close, or enmeshed with whom? Who is too distant, disengaged with another?

There are other ways that one can describe these characteristics. Boundaries is one of them. Enmeshment can be seen as overly permeable boundaries, while disengagement is the opposite. The notion of boundaries tends to be a more therapeutic one, since boundary making is a standard technique of structural family therapy while the terms "enmeshment" and "disengagement" are more descriptive.

The parameters of proximity and distance are always gauged against the developmental stage and relationships of the individuals involved in order to ascertain whether the system is functional or dysfunctional. In other words, what would be deemed to be appropriate concern, attention, and involvement between a mother and a 3-year-old would be termed "enmeshment" when this same involvement occurred between a mother and an 18-year-old. Conversely, a young woman who is left to her own devices at age 18 by her parents would be considered to be grossly neglected if the same interpersonal distance were to occur between her and her spouse. The latter would be termed "disengagement."

So "enmeshment" and "disengagement" are relative to the developmental stage of the individual. In a sense, what we are describing is the family in two dimensions: time and space. One coordinate is the chronological and developmental stage of the family members, while the other parameter is "space," the degrees of proximity and distance between family members within and between subsystems.

After gauging the amount of proximity and distance between family members, the therapist compares the family's configuration with a clinically derived conceptualization of the functional family. This model of the normal family shares with organizational theory the notion that, to be functioning well, an organization must have clearly defined lines of autonomy and responsibility. The well functioning family must have optimal amounts of subsystem integrity. That is, the parental, spouse, sibling, individual, family—all subsystems—must be protected by a boundary which is appropriate to the developmental stage of the individuals involved. For example, mother should not be closer to her 15-year-old child than to her spouse. Conversely, father should not be more proximate with his mother than with his wife. An individual should have enough interpersonal distance in order to develop competence and skills, but family members still need sufficient care and protection to be safe and they need to be supported in exploring alternatives.

These are, of course, circular definitions. Just how is "optimal" determined? The clinician answers this question in an empirical manner. Although therapists necessarily have a mental schema for "normal," their expertise is with dysfunctional families.

The structural therapist scans for areas of boundary dysfunction. For example, in the Williams family, mother regularly discussed father's drinking binges with Billy. This represents a boundary problem since father's alcohol usage is an area of conflict between husband and wife that should be handled between them. Another boundary problem was manifested by Billy, who almost invariably intervened when mother and father began to fight. And a final example is the way the family handled Billy's school problems. Mother and father spent every evening with the youngster, trying to get him to do his work. Indeed, the boy's homework had become everyone's homework.

Clinical acumen is required to read the structure from the clinical data. In this area, clinicians must be both observant and committed to their therapeutic stance, since, in our conceptualization, data is elicited by the active participation of the therapist.

Beatrice L. Wood (1981) demarcated the following parameters as indicative of proximity:

Contact time, the sheer amount of time spent together and the way the time is spent. For example, an isolated father and 14-year-old son spend all day Saturday and Sunday together, even though both are isolated from peers. In the therapy room, increased contact time is manifest by people having eye contact, talking, showing great interest in one another, often to the exclusion of others.

Personal space, defined as the area immediately surrounding the body and including the body, is one of the most private of preserves and the sharing of this space reflects a closeness not usually permitted to or by strangers or even acquaintances, in our society, unless under extenuating circumstances. Extreme examples of this aspect of enmeshment are frequently seen in child abusing families, where family members often invade one another's personal space. In less extreme situations, a parent may be talking while resting an elbow on a child, as though he or she were a prop. Family members' bodies are treated as contiguous, sharing the common family protoplasm.

Emotional space is frequently intruded upon in enmeshed families. If one member is sad, everybody is sad. Laughter, clowning, joking, and play are kinds of shared emotional experience. One delinquent boy and his father, who is estranged from his wife, became irate when the mother rebuked the boy in the therapy session, saying, "Billy and I cry for each other."

Information space is a parameter that is shared according to the amount and kind of contact time, although it is also possible for families to spend a great deal of time together in goal directed or play activity without sharing thoughts, feelings, or opinions. A common example of this is where family members are "memory banks" for one another.

Conversation space is defined by Wood (1981) as "the sharing of private conversations apart from other family members." The extent to which these kinds of interactions take place reflects the differentiation of proximity within the family. A frequent indicator of more functional families is whether teenagers can meet together without the parents present and criticize their folks.

Decision space pertains to how decisions are made. Whether they are made by individuals, or by subsystems, or by the entire family, gives much data regarding the structure. For example, in order for the parents in one anorectic family to have fights, they were forced to lock themselves in the bathroom, away from their 14-year-old daughter. Otherwise, she intruded and prevented them from resolving the issue.

As a clinician, one looks at such things as the parameters enumerated by Wood (1981) as well as innumerable other small bits of interaction. For example, Billy and mother each pull out a handkerchief in unison, so that they look almost choreographed, and go through a nose-blowing ritual lasting about 5 minutes. Or, in another family, the elderly widow invites her adult son to come "home" and live with her, "I'll cook for you." The adolescent boy and his mother who, as the therapist is challenging the system, says, "Mom, I'm thinking what you're thinking." Each interaction is weighed against a mental schema, based on clinical and personal experience, of what is appropriate for the developmental stage of the people involved.

Any one of these bits of data is, by itself, ambiguous and inconclusive. What is essential, of course, is the repetition of interaction into patterns that connect the transactions. The specific data that the structural family therapist uses to ascertain structure have been described at length, in publications (Minuchin, 1974; Minuchin & Fishman, 1981) as well as in numerous teaching tapes.

THE OBSERVER AS PART OF THE SYSTEM

The structure/developmental assessment rendered by the therapist is clinically based and therefore imprecise and impressionistic. The validity of the therapist's conceptualization is determined by making a therapeutic probe based on the hypothesis and following the feedback from the system. Does the probe lead to more transactions consistent with the hypothesis, or, to transformation of the system? Thus, to assess a system the therapist must probe it. But once we probe a system, we are to some extent a part of it.

From the systemic point of view, diagnosis in the traditional sense is not a viable concept, since it implies that there is a separation between the person doing the assessing and the "thing out there." In fact, the person doing the assessing is affecting the system being evaluated and vice versa. In Sal Minuchin's terms, the therapist is "right in the soup" with the family.

Carl Whitaker and Thomas Malone, in their book *Roots of Psychotherapy* (1981), suggested that in psychotherapy there is a merging of the therapist and patient. In the process a new entity is created: the therapeutic system. From this point of view, no longer can therapists talk of the patient the way the neatly dressed gentlemen in Rembrandt's painting, "The Anatomist," sitting around the cadaver, could discuss their findings. Instead, we are confronted with a relativistic world in which doctor and patient, matter and energy, and Yeats' dancer and dance become mutually interdependent.

By current ways of thinking, a generation later, the Whitaker and Malone (1981) insight seems intuitively obvious and almost a cliché. But it is a concept with profound implications. By their viewpoint, the therapist cannot *not* be some part of the system. The degree of involvement may vary according to how greatly we can resist induction by the family; nevertheless, in the process of therapy, the family and therapist form a unit.

The important and provocative question, both clinically and theoretically, is how to exploit this connection between therapist and family. Clinicians have struggled against this connectedness and numerous techniques have been evolved to minimize how well we are joined to the system: the two-way mirror, the strategic teams, cotherapists. But none of these is practical for most therapeutic situations. Furthermore, by strenuously bolstering the separation between the family and the therapist, valuable opportunities to produce change are being missed.

The structural therapist makes use of the inevitability of becoming part of the family system by utilizing a specific intervention, the therapeutic probe.

Varela states that "the invariance that characterizes the system can only be studied under perturbations that reveal it" (Varela, 1979). Thus, the therapist, in Varela's words, perturbs the system.

Through this perturbation, the therapist gets essential diagnostic information about structure. According to Varela, "The outcome of a perturbation—a compensation—reflects the organization and structure of the system; the outcome of an input reflects a structure attributed both to the environment and the internal operation of the system" (Varela, 1979). Thus, the therapist probes, and the way the system reacts reflects the internal dynamic or structure of the system.

In cybernetic terms, we can diagram this conceptualization:

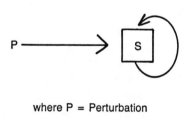

where P = Perturbation
S = System

The therapist, through the therapeutic probe or perturbation, acts upon the system. The system reacts according to its own rules or internal dynamic, hence the arrow. The term Ashby (1956) uses to describe a system such as this is "semi-isolated." Perturbations affect the system, but the ensuing behavior reveals the internal dynamic, or structure, of the system. This diagram reflects a system where the therapist is outside.

Essentially, every family presents the "Problem of the Black Box" which refers to a situation where an electrical engineer is given a sealed box with terminals for input. By varying the input, the worker must determine the content of the box (Ashby, 1956). The perturbations of the system are the input utilized by the structural therapist to ascertain the "content," or the *structure,* of the black box, or family. (*Perturbation* is used here in its most general sense. Varela and Maturana use this term in a very specific sense to indicate an observer who is only outside of a system ["A finger pushing a balloon" (Keeney, 1982)]. The term is used in this article to indicate perturbation resulting from an observer who is either inside *or* outside of the system.)

For example, at the moment the therapist supports the mother in her desire to have her 9-year-old go to school, the little girl and her grandmother look at each other and, almost in unison, say, "But she [mother] wants me to go to that Muslim school." Hence, the therapist has elicited data regarding the structure: the youngster and grandmother have a coalition.

In an anorectic family, the family was asked to eat lunch as usual. The anorectic refused to eat. The therapist tells the family, "Your daughter has to eat or she'll die." In response, mother said, "You've got to eat," and held the sandwich up to the girl's mouth. Father, slouching in his chair, said, "Don't shout . . . do you want some black coffee?" Through the perturbation, the parents, who previously appeared unified, were revealed to be divided.

Probing further, the therapist supports the father, at which point mother and daughter become angry, revealing their coalition. Deciding to probe further, the therapist continues to support father. Then, something odd happens: the therapist finds himself supporting mother, even though he had intended to continue bolstering father.

The clinician had become inducted. The family has certain preferred alternatives. One of these is to support mother, who is central, over father, who is distant and peripheral. Just like a tire slipping into a rut, the therapist, in spite of his or her intentions, is controlled by the context, the family, and follows the groove.

Thus, perturbation of the system by the therapist does not occur only with the therapist outside of the system. Instead, perturbation also occurs with the therapist inside the system. From this vantage point, another cybernetic schematic is more appropriate:

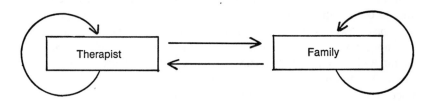

In short, both the therapist and the family are semi-isolated systems with each perturbing the other. Each system, then, responds to the feedback both by reacting according to its internal dynamic as well as by giving feedback to the other subsystem. The family, through its behavior, perturbs the therapist who is, of course, also a subsystem. The therapist then reacts according to his or her own internal dynamic. Thus, a relationship emerges which is the coupling of these two semi-isolated systems.

An important question is, to what degree does the subjective experience of the therapist reflect relevant data about the therapeutic system? Or, conversely, does the therapist's experience of a family essentially represent his or her own internal dynamic (that is, countertransference) and hence does he or she reveal more about the clinician than about the family?

In structural therapy one makes the assumption that the therapist's subjective experiences provide important data about the system. Thus, the therapist does not fight his or her reactions. On the contrary, one allows, and even closely attends to, the internal experience during a session, since these impressions are a source of relevant information about the system.

This is not to say that therapists do not bring their own real-life problems and areas of conflict to therapy. Inevitably, these conflicts or classical countertransference issues occur, but they are not pervasive. Instead, in certain touchy areas the therapist needs to be cautious. A therapist who is going through a divorce, having children leave home, or having experienced the recent death of a family member would, needless to say, have to be careful with families that present with similar difficulties. But these danger areas are the exception, not the rule. At other times the therapist can utilize his or her own responses to perturbations of the system as more data, which elucidate the structure of the family.

In essence, what I am suggesting is that in the situation represented by the second diagram, there is greater weight to the perturbation of the therapist (lower arrow) than to his or her internal dynamic, which is set off in response to the perturbation. Thus the structural therapist makes the assumption that his or her subjective reaction provides important data about the system. The therapist, therefore, can allow himself to experience subjective reaction as the session unfolds.

> As the Williams family comes in, the therapist's reaction to the father is that he is weak and incompetent. This may be seen as inducted by the system. The therapist increases intensity in an attempt to increase the closeness between mother and father. At one point, he has the fantasy that the father will collapse. This is also inducted by the system. Now that the child has improved, the therapist becomes convinced that the father is too weak to be interested in working on his marriage or be available to his wife. The therapist has fallen into the family's rut.

This question brings us back to the quotes by Tolstoy and Bateson. Indeed, families and systems are both verbs, changing constantly. As Shands says, there is built-in contradiction in naming (or, for that matter, diagnosis) since naming ostensibly refers to something stable when what one is describing is constantly involved in metamorphosis and transmutation (Shands, 1971). Yet families do fall into patterns at a given point in time. Nevertheless, we stand the risk in the process of assessing a family, of reifying, and thereby stabilizing, the very family organization that we are attempting to change. In order to avoid this reification, the therapist must convert the contradiction to a paradox, that is, a contradiction that works and is intrafunctional: How can we name without impeding the process of the system?

But this very dilemma, whether we stand the risk in the process of assessing a family of interfering with the family as "a verb," assumes a division between the therapist and the family. Instead, if we assume the therapist is an integral part of the therapeutic system, then the very process of naming is one more characteristic of the system since it is evolved from it. Hence, the process of diagnosis is a legitimate systemic phenomenon, one more manifestation of the family's patterning those who contact it. Thus, the family inducts the therapist to come across such a diagnosis. Hence there is a complementarity between the organization of the therapeutic system and the evaluation and diagnosis of the observer.

As the family interacts with the therapist, the following occurs. The family, connected to the therapist, pulls forth certain reactions. These can be the subjective experience of the therapist as described above, or, pulled from the therapist, can be an assessment or a description of pattern. Now, traditional psychiatric diagnostic categories are counterproductive because they see the family as a static entity. Such traditional diagnosis results in a family being fixed, like a collector's butterflies.

But does diagnosis in structural family therapy more accurately reflect the input from the therapeutic system than the traditional psychiatric evaluation?

The answer, frankly, is probably not. Naming is always on a different level of abstraction than the process of the family and hence may be complementary to the process, but only distantly so.

THE OBSERVER BOTH INSIDE AND OUTSIDE THE SYSTEM

Structural family therapy, unlike most other family therapies, relies heavily on the enactment in the therapy session of interactions between family members. During these scenarios, the therapist often tries to be as decentralized as possible, striving to be the audience/director of the therapeutic drama and only selectively entering the fray. This technique allows the therapist to ascertain if the transactions follow the pattern that he or she has hypothesized since interactions occur in a more naturalistic manner.

Of course, the therapist, once joined to the system, is always affecting the flow of interactions in some way.

Billy says to his father, "I don't like you. You're not really part of this family." The therapist, surprised by the bristling hostility, sits up straighter in his chair and stares at the mother, who sits implacably still.

Mother ignores the state of the therapist, but father, shamed, gets angrier.

So here we have two components described above: The therapist's anger, reflecting his internal dynamic, having two "spirited" older school-age kids at home; and, second, the impinging of the system on the clinician. As an outsider, he slipped into the family's rut and was inducted into father's position, that of the outsider. Hence, he was inducted by the system to unknowingly take the linear position of seeing father as a victim.

For purposes of evaluation, it is important to observe the subjective experience as described above, as well as to note the structure that was revealed in spite of the therapist's participation by the enactment. In essence, during an evaluation the structural family therapist vacillates between the situations depicted in the two diagrams.

Every enactment represents a probe that reveals the internal dynamic of the black box. Also, the therapist who inevitably participates in some way in a feedback loop, provides and receives data that reveal important information about the larger system, family plus therapist. With enactment and the therapist's ability to become decentralized, the clinician is able to synthesize the two positions, the family as a verb and the family as falling into a recognizable pattern. At once the therapist can observe the family's patterns as they evolve in the therapy room, and at the same time experience firsthand the pushes and pulls of the family dance. In a sense, we are describing two simultaneously contradictory definitions of the system. One includes the therapist observer, and the other excludes the therapist observer.

At once, the therapist is both inside and outside of the system. If a therapist cannot attain this eminently ambiguous position, as every clinician knows, then he or she is in danger of either going off the "deep end" and being extruded by the family as an outsider, or off the "shallow end" by being too well joined and hence hopelessly inducted by the family.

In a sense, to use an analogy from painting, via enactment, the clinician is capable of a cubist solution to this dilemma.

> In cubism the forms are broken down into a series of sharply angled or faceted planes. Traditionally, the painter views his subject from one static position outside the picture frame . . . [The cubists] on the other hand, disintegrate the form into a series of simultaneously viewed but different aspects of the same subject . . . [To achieve greater understanding or analysis of the figure, the cubist] steps into the picture frame and walks about the subject, observing it from various angles (Myers, 1967).

No longer does the therapist have to rely on a flat, two dimensional representation such as in a Giotto. He or she does not need to lose, in a blaze of motion, like Jackson Pollock, all form. Instead, like a Braque or

Picasso, the therapist can observe the subject from different angles, and experience simultaneously the contradictory aspects of the family as both a verb and a noun.

REFERENCES

Ashby, W.R. *Design for a brain.* London: Chapman & Hall, 1952.

Ashby, W.R. *An introduction to cybernetics.* London: Chapman & Hall, 1956.

Bateson, G. *Mind and nature.* New York: Dutton, 1979.

Kaufmann, W. (Ed.) *Hegel, texts and commentary.* New York: Anchor, 1965.

Keeney, B. Personal communication, March 1982.

Maturana, H.R. Biology of language: The epistemology of reality. In C.A. Miller & E. Lenneberg (Eds.), *Psychology and biology of language and thought.* New York: Academic, 1978.

Minuchin, S. *Families and family therapy.* Cambridge, Mass.: Harvard, 1974.

Minuchin, S. Personal communication, February 1978.

Minuchin, S. Taming monsters. Philadelphia Child Guidance Clinic, Videotape Rental Library.

Minuchin, S. & Fishman, H.C. *Family therapy techniques.* Cambridge, Mass.: Harvard, 1981.

Montalvo, B. A family with a little fire. Philadelphia Child Guidance Clinic, Videotape Rental Library.

Myers, B.S. *Art and civilization.* New York: McGraw-Hill, 1967.

Selvini Palazzoli, M. Personal communication, February 1982.

Shands, H.C. *The war with words.* The Hague: Mouton, 1971.

Varela, F. *Principles of biological anatomy.* New York: North Holland, 1979.

Whitaker, C.W. Personal communication, January 1982.

Whitaker, C.W., & Malone, T.P. *Roots of psychotherapy.* New York: Brunner Mazel, 1981.

Wood, B.L., Unpublished doctoral dissertation. University of Pennsylvania, 1981.

4. The Family and Public Service Systems: An Assessment Method

Evan Imber Coppersmith, Ph.D.
Training Coordinator
Family Therapy Program
Associate Professor
Department of Psychiatry
Faculty of Medicine
University of Calgary
Calgary, Alberta, Canada

The author expresses her appreciation to doctoral students in family therapy at the University of Massachusetts. Their contributions in the seminar "The Family and Larger Systems" and their commitment to working in the public sector with families intensely involved with larger systems helped shape the issues addressed in this article.

Four

THE PROBLEM

Mother: *(speaking to the family therapist)*
Caroline needs to come home with me. She needs discipline and to learn to obey my rules.

Youth Advocate: *(who brought Caroline, age 16, to the session, from the youth shelter where she was staying, and entered the session uninvited)*
Caroline is a young *adult*. She wants individual therapy, and I think her wishes should be respected.

Welfare Worker: *(who had a long-standing professional relationship with the mother, a single parent, and smiled at her as he spoke)*
Caroline and her mother need to express their deep-seated emotions toward each other. They're very angry at one another.

DURING THIS BRIEF BUT INTENSE INTERCHANGE CAROLINE, who had been anorectic for over a year, and had been shuttling between several foster homes and her own home, sat staring at the floor. When the family therapist attempted to ask her a question, she looked around at her mother, the advocate, and the welfare worker, and then bolted from the room. The advocate went after her, and the mother and the welfare worker consoled each other.

Many families, like the one described above, exist in enduring relationships with public service systems, including schools, hospitals, welfare, probation, youth agencies, foster care, and the courts. Several problems may arise from this kind of involvement. It is not uncommon for these systems to be in unrecognized or unacknowledged conflict with one another regarding their goals and choice of treatment for clients (Coppersmith, 1982; Hoffman & Long, 1969; Selig, 1976). Various public service systems frequently bring competing points of view to bear on a family's problem and its preferred solution. Several "languages" (e.g., legal, educational, medical, and psychological) may be spoken by representatives of agencies involved with a family, promoting all of the clarity of the Tower of Babel. The simultaneous diagnosis of a child as "bad," "mad," and "sick" is not unusual. One or more family members may become intensely involved with a probation officer, a teacher, or a physician, in ways that may inadvertently handicap the family's problem solving capacities (Goolishian & Anderson, 1981; Palazzoli, Boscolo, Cecchin, & Prata, 1980a, 1980b). Mutual expectations between the family and helping systems may be widely asynchronous, resulting in a spiraling cycle of blame, disappointment, and distance (Bell & Zucker, 1968). Some families, characterized by what Wynne and Singer (1963, 1965) called a "rubber fence," absorb and neutralize myriad numbers of helpers. At times, such helpers may struggle with each other, while the family either stands by and watches, or family members line up allies in a community-wide tug of war! In one recent case of a conflicted and mutually abusing couple, the wife had four agencies on her side, and the husband had four agencies on his side. The agencies' struggles with each other mirrored those of the couple.

The problem facing the family therapist working with families who are intensely involved with social agencies has been recognized by a number of practitioners in recent years (Coppersmith, 1982; Goolishian & Anderson, 1981; Haley, 1980; Hoffman & Long, 1969). Haley states, "The unit for the therapist . . . consists of the family *and* professionals involved" (1980, p. 61). A small literature is developing that highlights the problem and suggests interventions (Goolishian & Anderson, 1981; Palazzoli et al., 1980a, 1980b). The present work is a contribution to that literature, focusing on the family therapist's necessary task of assessing the family's relationship to larger systems prior to intervention.

THE ASSESSMENT METHOD

Who Is Involved?

Several aspects of the relationship between the family and other systems may be of critical importance to the work of the family therapist. This work begins, however, with a simple list:

- Who are the larger systems presently involved with the family?
- How many agencies regularly interact with the family?
- How long-standing or how recent is the relationship?

Gathering such information immediately begins to provide the skeletal features of an ecosystemic map. Is this a family where one member is intensely involved with one outside helper, who has become "a member of the family" (Goolishian & Anderson, 1981; Palazzoli et al., 1980a, 1980b)? Or, rather, is this a family with a long history of being passed from one agency to another with no hint of change? Has the family rapidly enlisted a dozen or more agencies? The length and chronicity of this list forms the family therapist's conceptualization of the problem.

Definitions of the Problem

The next step is to determine how the family and the various helping systems are defining the problem. Do the family and larger systems even agree that there *is* a problem for which family therapy is an appropriate response? Is a symmetrical battle ensuing regarding the nature of the problem?

This kind of problem definition illuminates each participant's preferred locus of blame. For example, the school may say "it's mother's fault," while at the same time, the family unites to blame the teacher.

The question "whose problem is it, anyway?", especially crucial when a family has been *sent* to therapy by others, begins to be answered when the family therapist notices, for instance, that the outside systems are far more upset or worried than the family members.

An index of optimism and pessimism regarding the efficacy of the therapeutic process emerges. One may discover that all involved believe the problem to be solvable. More likely, the family therapist may find that family and agencies differ significantly on this issue and escalate conflict over "who knows best." Furthermore, it may be that the probation department, the welfare department, and the public school all define the problem as "hopeless" and the family members agree, and are setting about to use family therapy as one more link in a chain of self-fulfilling prophecies.

Nature of the Relationship

As one ascertains the definitions of the problem, the nature of the relationships between family and agency begins to unfold. Any, or all, of four major areas may perpetuate rather than alleviate a family's problem. These include

- mutual myths
- family–larger system boundaries
- triads
- previous attempted solutions

Just as a family has myths about itself, so families and larger systems have myths regarding one another that often preserve the status quo. A family may view agencies and their representatives as "beneficent," "harmful," "meddling," "useless," "wasteful," "threatening," etc. Families who have had a long history of involvement with outside agencies frequently hold the same point of view toward all helpers, so that any new helper is immediately defined by the family's agreed upon myth. A family therapist who enters a family that holds negative myths about helpers must quickly discern the myth and find a way to jar loose this point of view, or run the risk of being yet another name on the family's list of "worthless outsiders." Simultaneously, the social service system develops myths about particular families as "unworkable," "uncooperative," "hostile," "pitiable," etc. These myths are often communicated among several agencies involved with a family. The expectations of those to whom a family is referred are easily colored.

Case Example 1

A family was referred for therapy due to the obstreperous behavior of the 7-year-old daughter. During the referral process, the therapist learned that school personnel viewed the family as "irresponsible." The family, in turn, described the school as "intimidating and disrespectful." The two most important systems in the little girl's life were in a war with one another, and the child's behavior was the ready battlefield. The more the school criticized the child in terms that blamed the parents, the more the parents came to her defense, and the worse her behavior became in the school setting, initiating a new cycle of blame and defense. The intense and frustrating interaction of family and school, which became the focus of the therapy, was readily apparent to the therapist who heard their mutual myths.

The boundaries between a family and larger systems may be too diffuse, handicapping the family's own coping resources, or too rigid, preventing the utilization of needed assistance. When family–agency boundaries are diffuse, frequently the agency will define the family's problems for it, become entangled in aspects of the family's life that are not the purview of the particular agency, and alternate between overprotecting family members and becoming exasperated with them. Rigid boundaries may be characterized by a family's stereotyped denial of entry to other systems, and isolation from extrafamilial sources of information.

The number of outside systems engaged with a family may not necessarily indicate the nature of family–agency boundaries. A family may be involved with only one system—for instance, welfare—and yet that system may have intruded into a widening circle of concerns in the life of the family. Conversely, a family may have 10 agencies knocking at its door, but manage to frustrate the efforts of each.

The triadic combinations among families and larger systems are legion, involving alliances and splits between whole families and whole agencies, individual family members and various agencies, and among several larger systems. An examination of families who were chronically involved with public agencies over several generations revealed that such families were part of enduring triads, characterized either by conflictual relationships among the several systems "helping" the family, or between the family itself and an agency (Harrell, 1980). The three triadic patterns defined by Minuchin (1974, 1978), *detour, cross-generational coalition,* and *triangulation,* are useful to assess family–larger system relationships.

In *detour,* one may see otherwise conflictual larger systems unite to attack or overprotect a family or one of its members. Additionally, one may see family members be able to submerge their own conflicts by focusing on an outside agency.

Case Example 2

A couple was in conflict for many years, but united to attack their teen-age son, who, in turn, gave them frequent cause to be angry. At

18 the son left the house. In the next six months, the husband and wife each engaged with a large number of outside helping agencies. Each engagement *began* with subtle complaints about the other spouse and then rapidly moved to both spouses uniting to attack the helper as "incompetent." The helping systems in this case had inadvertently stepped into the void left by the absent son, with the result that there was no change in the spouse relationship.

A version of what Minuchin refers to as *cross-generational coalition,* perhaps better renamed as *cross-system coalition,* may be seen when individual family members form alliances with members of outside systems. Such alliances either exclude or are patently against other family members, and may exacerbate problems in the family. A frequently seen cross-system coalition is that of one spouse and a "helper" that focuses on the shortcomings of the other spouse. Another common arrangement is that of a youth worker intensely allied with an adolescent against his "old-fashioned" parents. Possible solutions within the family are short-circuited by the potential for disloyalty to the cross-system alliance.

Case Example 3

A family was referred for therapy by the juvenile probation department due to the increasingly delinquent behavior of the 15-year-old son. It was determined in the first session that the boy had alliances with two youth workers and a school counselor. Whenever the parents attempted to set rules for the boy, or discipline him for breaking rules, the boy would complain to the youth workers and counselor. They, in turn, would telephone the parents and reprimand them for not treating the boy as a "young adult." By the time therapy was initiated, the parents felt hopeless and disgusted with outside helpers, and the boy's escalating delinquency was defined by larger systems as proof that he required two workers and a counselor!

Finally, in *triangulation,* a family may exist in two incompatible alliances with larger systems, which are in conflict with one another. The larger systems may fight over the definitions of the family's problem and the preferred solution. If the family is in some way required to be involved with both systems (e.g., welfare and public school), it may find itself in a fierce loyalty bind, not unlike the triangulation of two parents and a child.

Foster care, in particular, easily engenders triangulation among natural parents, foster parents, case worker, and child. Lack of clarity regarding who provides guidance for the child often results in the child attempting to make adult decisions. Escalation over "who knows best" generally leads to an untenable position for the child, as he or she cannot be loyal to his or her natural parents without being disloyal to the foster parents, and vice versa.

The family and larger systems may form triadic patterns that inadvertently perpetuate distress. The problems that one assumes are internal to the family play a crucial function in a number of relationships between the family and agencies, and among the agencies themselves.

The solution behavior of various agencies involved with a family may exacerbate difficulties and contribute to a cycle of "more of the same wrong solution" (Watzlawick, Weakland, & Fisch, 1974). Asking a family what has been tried may reveal that the "solution" has been to involve more and more agencies, or that the "solution" has been to put an outside adult helper in charge of determining the rules for a child, thus disempowering the parents, or that the "solution" has involved labeling the problem in ways that engender chronicity and long-term treatment (e.g., hyperactivity, manic-depression, etc.). Useful solutions may have been tried and discarded too quickly, or offered in language not appropriate to the family's frame of reference.

How To Assess

The Stance of the Therapist

The family therapist who is working with families involved with public sector systems is faced with the complex task of creating and maintaining multiple relationships, while avoiding unplanned alliances and splits. At the beginning of any such therapy, both family and larger system come with particular expectations of the family therapist.

If the family has been involved with agencies for a long time, the family therapist is generally considered to be "more of the same." If public systems have historically engaged with and given up on family members, the family enters therapy anticipating that the therapist will do likewise. Often such families will set up trials for the therapist, designed to test the therapist's tolerance. If the family's experience with agencies is one where helpers have given lots of advice and gradually taken over role functions for family members, they may try to influence the family therapist to do the same.

If the family is currently embroiled in a struggle with the very agency that has referred the family for therapy, they may move swiftly to engage the therapist in an alliance, while the referral source is doing the same. The therapist may be pressured by the agencies to view the family as "uncooperative" while at the same time pulled by the family to view the agencies as "the enemy." The stage for triangulation of the therapist is thus set.

To be effective, the family therapist must seek to create *unexpected* relationships with both family and larger systems. The meta level position of "neutrality," as described by Palazzoli et al., in which "the therapist is allied with everyone and no one at the same time" (1980b, p. 11) allows the therapist to be effective with the family without alienating the larger system, and vice versa. Therapists must expand this neutrality beyond their behavior in actual sessions, to include all of the between session action that tends to occur when working with families and larger systems. This entails the very powerful detriangulating move of refusing to be the keeper of secrets. Agency reports about families should be communicated to the family in clear, demystifying terms. Negative points of view about the family on the part of larger systems should become "grist for the mill" in family therapy sessions in ways that lead to rapprochement, rather than escalating anger. Responses to agency requests for reports on the family should be the joint creation of the therapist and family. The author is especially appreciative to Dr. Linda Webb-Woodard for developing an approach that makes families partners, rather than subjects, in reports that can affect their futures.

For the family and agencies to begin to have a new and more satisfying experience with one another requires that the family therapist feel unconstrained by professional allegiances and by the basically condescending desire to "protect" the family. If potent family therapy is the art of coalitions (Haley, 1976), then working with the family and public sector systems in ways that enhance both and estrange neither is the pièce de résistance.

Gathering the Information

The family therapist needs to gather information regarding the interaction of family and agencies in ways that shed light on those dimensions of the relationship that either inadvertently support family distress or obviate therapeutic intervention. Several sources of information are readily apparent to the therapist who is purposeful in attending to the interplay of family and larger system.

If a family is referred by a larger system, the nature of the referral will begin to provide clues for the therapist. Does the referral source describe the family in mythical terms? Is the referral a dare to succeed where the agency has failed? Does the representative of a larger system attempt to "gossip" about the family members, describing aspects of the family's life that are beyond his or her appropriate vantage point? Is the tone of reports sent about the family negative and hopeless? Has the referring agency cajoled, threatened, or ordered the family to therapy? Will the larger system now exit from the family's life, or will contact be maintained? If contact is ongoing, will the action of family therapy sessions be a focus of discussion between a helper and a family member? Are social agencies paying for the therapy, and, hence, expecting to "own" the outcomes? Telephone calls, letters, and reports from agencies to the family therapist, whether invited or uninvited, provide answers to some of these questions, and begin to inform the therapist's thinking regarding myths, boundaries, triads, and previous solution behavior.

The larger systems' involvement with a family is often more apparent than the family's involvement with larger systems. If a family requests therapy, no mention may be made of relationships with public sector systems. This is especially the case if alliances are covert, or if the family is expert at inviting in outsiders while warding off their impact. It behooves the family therapist to inquire about larger systems at *every* initial interview. The author was requested to consult on a case where therapy had been ongoing for four months. The family situation was deteriorating. The therapist had assumed no outside agency involvement in this upper middle class, professionally employed family. The consultant suggested devoting the next session to this issue. No fewer than eight agencies, taking sides with one parent or the other, were discovered to be part of this family's "meaningful system."

If the therapist discovers family–larger system relationships, then the therapist must determine the "meaningful system" involved in patterns that support or intensify family difficulty. This assessment often requires inviting representatives of agencies to one or more family therapy sessions. Just as one invites family members to sessions in ways that do not impart blame, so one must include agency personnel in ways that suggest all are needed to solve the problem. The family therapist is in the precarious position of establishing leadership in the session in such a way that the therapist neither provokes the larger system representative to compete, nor loses the family's trust in the therapist's capabilities to guide the session. The session conduct described by Palazzoli et al. (1980b) and referred to as "circularity" enables the family therapist to include agency personnel at sessions with families in a way that is at once respectful and informative, and which *implicitly* reframes the family's problem as one that will require a shift in family–larger system relations for its solution. The nature of the family–agency relationship comes into full relief in sessions focusing on such circular questions as:

1. Who has been the most helpful in working on this problem? And then who? etc.

(Content and analogic responses to this question quickly reveal alliances and splits.)

2. Who is the most upset by the problem? And then who? etc.

Here the therapist is able to discern who "owns" the problem. Is the agency person overinvolved, while family members smile silently at one another? Are mother and teacher very upset, while father and son minimize the issue?

3. If the problem were to be solved, what would people be concerned about?

This question will indicate whether the larger systems and the family envision disengaging from one another, or finding some new areas through which to maintain involvement. Do, for instance, the adolescent and his youth advocate begin to appear very depressed during this discussion?

4. When this problem occurs, whom are you most likely to turn to? And then who? etc.

Responses here will inform the therapist regarding boundaries, alliances, and myths between the family and larger systems. Additionally, how the agency and family are defining the problem, as well as their potential reliance on systems other than the family for solving the family's problem, will become clear.

As an example, a welfare worker who responds: "When this problem occurs, I would call his probation officer" is defining the problem as legal, involving delinquency, and placing its solution outside the family. Another worker might answer the same question, regarding the same circumstances, with: "I would call the psychiatrist and request an evaluation for medication,'' thus defining the issue as medical and locating the solution again outside the family. A parent may indicate that he would turn to the school counselor *before* turning to his wife.

The family therapist should enter an initial session with a family and larger system representatives with a series of such questions in mind, tailored to fit the specific circumstances of the case.

Intervention as Assessment

When one employs a systems perspective, many assessment questions are only answered by the process of intervening. The flexibility or rigidity of family–larger system relationships, the ease or difficulty of searching for new options, and the potential for systemic transformation all become more visible when the therapist actually intervenes in the complex network of family–larger system. Responses to interventions inform the therapist about the nature of myths, boundaries, and triads. Does the therapist, immediately following initial positive changes in the family, that include mother turning more to her husband for support and less to the school, receive a telephone call from a teacher complaining about the child's behavior from three weeks earlier? Are the family therapist's attempts to shore up the family's boundaries to the outside world met by the welfare worker referring the family for two new services? As family functioning improves, do the larger systems distance themselves appropriately, behave punitively, or widen their circle of concerns? Are the agencies able to recognize and affirm the family's development through time, or are outmoded points of view still held and allowed to guide actions? Two brief case examples may serve to illustrate how intervention feeds back on assessment.

Case Example 4

A family, whose adolescent son was in long-term foster care due to abuse that had ceased two years earlier, was referred for therapy by a probation officer. At the first session, the parents complained bitterly about their situation. They were doing well with their other children and believed the conditions surrounding the abuse were no longer present. They were especially hurt and angry that their son seemed to prefer his welfare worker to them. The probation officer and the welfare worker were invited to the next session. During the session it became clear that the probation officer and the welfare worker had very different ideas about what was best for the family. The probation officer, convinced that his work with the parents had been successful, supported the boy's return to the home. The welfare worker, who spent several hours a week with the boy in various aspects of his foster care, counseling, and accompanying him on visits home, wanted him to remain in foster care for the foreseeable future. At the verbal level, family and larger systems expressed a wish to be through with one another, and agreed that the road to such disengagement began with the parents making rules for their son's visits home. As the parents began this task in a competent manner, the probation officer smiled smugly at the welfare worker. The parents made several rules appropriate for a 14-year-old, including a rule that they, rather than the welfare worker, would drive him to and from sessions. The session ended and the worker moved swiftly to ask the boy if he understood all of the rules. The boy nodded. The worker then implored the boy to realize that this meant she would not drive him home that night. The boy began to cry and insisted that he must go with the worker. A temper tantrum ensued in the waiting room. The probation officer and the welfare worker argued. The parents threw up their hands and drove off without their son.

The intervention of the parents setting rules—an intervention which, if successful, would begin to firm up the family's boundaries with outside systems, interdict the son–welfare worker alliance, and alter the symmetrical battle of probation and welfare—was met with immediate challenge and a return to the status quo. This intervention, nonetheless, provided a wealth of information regarding the nature of family–larger system relationships that could be useful in planning the next steps in the therapy. Most obvious was the potential trap of triangulation for the therapist.

Case Example 5

A family was referred for therapy by a pediatrician because of the increasingly unmanageable behavior of their 9-year-old daughter. The girl had been a problem for the family for several years because of her tantrums, lying, and learning difficulties in school. Physicians and school personnel had labeled her "hyperactive," and she was placed on medication. The family also referred to her as "hyperactive" whenever she was naughty.

At the end of the first session, the father complained that his experiences with professional helpers had been unsatisfactory largely because they "never shared information with us." Interaction with helpers had been the domain of the mother, aggravating an already tense relationship between the parents.

It was decided by the therapeutic team that a very different experience with helpers would be required in order to effectively alter family relationships. At the same time, careful assessment of school and medical interaction with the family indicated that the success of any change effort hinged on their cooperation. The intervention occurred in two steps. The first reframed the relationship of family-school-physician as a partnership required to solve the problem. This was very different from the previous subordinate position of the family vis-a-vis helpers. It also sent the message to the helpers that the problem could not be solved without them. The second step entailed getting all to agree to drop the label "hyperactive" and all its concomitant treatment, and to treat the girl as a normal girl who engaged in naughty behavior. This was a bold move, requiring different responses from all of the adults in the girl's life. In subsequent weeks, the physician became appropriately distanced from the family, since the girl no longer had a "medical" problem. The school teacher expected her to do her work and to behave well. When she misbehaved, she was sent to the principal like any other child. The father, who had been distant, and the mother, who had been busily engaged with helpers, moved toward one another. The little girl became, in her mother's words, a "normal, active 9-year-old."

Careful intervention, in this case, was responded to with flexibility by the family and larger systems. Long-standing relationships shifted profoundly.

CONCLUSION: THE PURPOSES OF ASSESSMENT

This article has detailed a method of assessing the complex relationships between families and larger systems. Four major purposes can be accomplished by the family therapist who attends to this critical aspect of the work.

First, the therapist can establish a *different* kind of relationship with the family from the kind they have learned to expect, mistrust, and ultimately neutralize with previous helpers. In the case discussed above, keen attention to the father's misgivings about "professionals talking to one another, but never to the family" contributed to the development of a therapeutic stance of openness with information and interventions that empowered the family as their own best resource.

Second, assessment may reveal significant points of entry into the family sphere. Families who are involved with multiple agencies, and who are being *sent* to family therapy, often see no use for yet one more professional intruding in their lives. Framing the family's problem as one of "too many outsiders" often engages the family with a therapeutic endeavor designed to enhance their functioning with the ultimate result that the larger systems will leave.

Third, assessing the relationship of the family and larger systems in the ways suggested here enables the family therapist to maintain viable relationships with agencies. Helpers in public sector systems frequently experience disconfirmation, both from clients and other professionals. This disconfirmation feeds cycles of symmetrical escalation and scapegoating. The family therapist, who can view family–larger system interaction as circular and often stuck in ways that none malevolently intend, is in a position to affirm the appropriate contributions of agencies and initiate "partnerships" in the service of the family.

Finally, careful consideration of family–larger system involvement clarifies those sequences that support distress. This knowledge informs strategic interventions designed to block or alter stereotyped patterns. Free from the characterizations of "villains" and "victims," the family therapist can set about the work of empowering the family to search for its own solutions.

REFERENCES

Bell, N., & Zucker, R. Family–hospital relationships in a state hospital setting: A structural-functional analysis of the hospitalization process. *The International Journal of Social Psychiatry,* 1968–69, *XV,* 73–80.

Coppersmith, E. The place of family therapy in the homeostasis of larger systems. In M. Aronson & R. Wolberg (Eds.), *Group and family therapy, 1982: An overview.* New York: Brunner Mazel, in press.

Goolishian, H., & Anderson, H. Including non-blood-related persons in family therapy. In A. Gurman (Ed.), *Questions and answers in the practice of family therapy.* New York: Brunner Mazel, 1981.

Haley, J. *Problem-solving therapy: New strategies for effective therapy.* San Francisco: Jossey-Bass, 1976.

Haley, J. *Leaving home: The therapy of disturbed young people.* New York: McGraw-Hill, 1980.

Harrell, F. Family dependency as a transgenerational process: An ecological analysis of families in crisis. Unpublished dissertation, University of Massachusetts, Amherst, 1980.

Hoffman, L., & Long, L. A systems dilemma. *Family Process,* 1969, *8,* 211–234.

Minuchin, S. *Families and family therapy.* Cambridge, Mass.: Harvard University Press, 1974.

Minuchin, S. *Psychosomatic families: Anorexia nervosa in context.* Boston: Harvard, 1978.

Palazzoli, M., Boscolo, L., Cecchin, G., & Prata, G. The problem of the referring person. *Journal of Marital and Family Therapy*, 1980a, *6*, 3-9.

Palazzoli, M., Boscolo, L., Cecchin, G., & Prata, G. Hypothesizing-circularity-neutrality. Three guidelines for the conductor of the session. *Family Process*, 1980b, *19*, 3-12.

Selig, A. The myth of the multi-problem family. *American Journal of Orthopsychiatry*, 1976, *46*, 526-531.

Watzlawick, P., Weakland, J., & Fisch, R. *Change: Principles of problem formation and problem resolution*. New York: Norton, 1974.

Wynne, L., & Singer, M. Thought disorders and the family relations of schizophrenics. *Archives of General Psychiatry*, 1963, *9*, 191-206; 1965, *12*, 187-212.

5. Family Assessment in a Problem Oriented Record

Karl Tomm, M.D., F.R.C.P.(C.)
Director
Family Therapy Program
Professor
Department of Psychiatry
Faculty of Medicine
The University of Calgary
Alberta, Canada

G.L. Sanders, M.D., F.R.C.P.(C.)
Associate Director
Family Therapy Program
Assistant Professor
Department of Psychiatry
Faculty of Medicine
The University of Calgary
Alberta, Canada

The authors wish to acknowledge the direct and indirect contributions of many professional colleagues and students in developing the record system described in this article. In particular, Alberta Mental Health Services provided continuing grant support and Dr. L.M. Wright offered helpful comments on an earlier draft.

Five

INTRODUCTION

THE FIELD OF FAMILY THERAPY HAS STRUGGLED WITH THE issue of diagnosis since its beginnings. Nathan Ackerman, in fact, chaired a meeting on family diagnosis in 1955 (cited in Broderick & Schroder, 1981). Although interest in family diagnosis and family classification has been persistent, the field has not yet produced any generally accepted family nosology.

Fisher (1977) reviewed 20 years of literature on family classification. He was able to identify six family clusters by comparing the existing schemata of family types. However, he came to the conclusion that the development of a single, prominent classification schema may be more restrictive than helpful and suggested a multidimensional approach. Benjamin (1974) and Olson, Sprenkle, and Russell (1979) have been working in the latter direction but their models are research based and seem too cumbersome to use in day to day clinical practice. More recently Hoffman (1980) summarized some of the currently popular methods of typing clinical families. These include symptom typologies (e.g., schizophrenic vs. anorectic families), structural typologies (e.g., enmeshed vs. disengaged families), and theoretical typologies (e.g., open vs. closed systems). All of these descriptions remain very general, however, and provide little guidance for the therapist working with a specific case.

In this article we propose an alternative approach to the problem of family diagnosis. We suggest that an emphasis on a method of continuous family assessment is more useful (in clinical practice) than an emphasis on family diagnosis. This may be achieved by developing an open ended and changing problem list rather than using a finite schema of family classification. We even suggest that the clinician's attempt to classify and diagnose may impede rather than enable the therapeutic process. A problem oriented approach to record keeping, which emphasizes dynamic family assessment, eliminates the need to arrive at a singular family diagnosis.

THE LIMITATIONS OF DIAGNOSIS

Diagnosis is defined as "the art of distinguishing one disease from another" or "the determination of the nature of a case of disease" (*Medical Dictionary*, 1965). These definitions imply clear distinctions between sickness and health and between one illness and another. However, given our present state of knowledge about interpersonal problems, the distinction between pathology and normalcy and between problem types in families appears to be far more arbitrary. In fact, the designation of interpersonal pathology is often based more on the act of seeking help than on the phenomenology of the problem itself. For instance, the work of Cuber and Harroff (1965) implies that the vast majority of nonreferred middle class couples have constricted, conflict-ridden, or zestless marriages. Yet these couples were regarded as successful in the community, not as having pathological marriages. Diagnostic distinctions are useful in the practice of physiological medicine because they often imply a specific course of medical intervention. However, a family diagnosis does not imply specific interventions. At best it may suggest a general direction for therapy. For example an "enmeshed family" needs help in defining interpersonal boundaries but the diagnosis of enmeshment does not provide direction as to how this should be done. Distinctions between one family type and another are less useful in suggesting a particular intervention than the events occurring in the immediate interview. Thus the notion of a family diagnosis is at too abstract a level to be of much practical value.

More significantly, however, the act of diagnostic labelling carries with it the risk of stabilizing the very problematic process it is hoping to eliminate. When a family system identifies a particular member as "bad" or "mad," a pattern of scapegoating is activated, which tends to stabilize the problematic deviation. Similarly, when a clinician and the community label the family with a diagnosis, communication patterns in this larger system may inadvertently conspire to stabilize the family's "deviation." A scapegoating family can easily become the therapeutic community's scapegoat.

Assigning a definitive diagnosis also increases the risk of narrowing the range of alternatives that the therapist may entertain. A diagnostic label predisposes clinicians to be selective in their observations. They do this in order to validate the hypothetical diagnosis. This process is essential to confirm a particular diagnosis. However, this same selective perception tends to mask incompatible data that are extremely important in order for the therapist to obtain a comprehensive and flexible understanding of the case. Of course, a good diagnostician continually struggles against this constrictive tendency. Nevertheless, this inadvertent effect of labelling continues to operate. The label also predisposes the therapist to consider primarily those interventions that are associated with that diagnosis. By focusing only on the usual treatment he or she implicitly precludes other possibilities that may be more applicable and appropriate in a particular situation. Each family and each situation is unique. The application of a diagnostic label reduces the therapist's responsiveness to this uniqueness.

A diagnostic understanding also promotes an orientation to problems as static entities or as fixed patterns. A dynamic systems understanding promotes a more flexible view. However, flexibility implies change and change requires reassessment. Continuous reassessment maintains flexibility and avoids the risks of diagnostic labelling. For these compelling reasons, we consider the "art of diagnosis" to be less useful in family therapy than a "method of assessment."

A PROBLEM ORIENTED RECORD

The context for our method of family assessment is the Problem Oriented Family Therapy Record (POFTR). The POFTR was developed in our Calgary program during the mid-1970s in order to promote more rigorous family assessment without constraining the therapist's intuitive spontaneity and creativity during the actual interview. This was achieved by demanding more professional discipline and conceptual rigor when documenting the case, that is, when completing the clinical record after the interview has been completed. As any beginning family therapist can easily attest, the amount of information provided by a family can be overwhelming, leaving one at a loss as to how to make sense of it all.

One major advantage of the problem oriented record is that the structure of the record and the method of documentation help organize information about the case and its management in a systematic and logical manner. In addition, the problem orientation helps the therapist maintain a clear focus on the core problematic issues in the family.

The problem oriented family therapy record (POFTR) was modelled after Weed's (1970) problem oriented medical record (POMR) and has the same basic structure. It is composed of four major parts: (1) Data Base, (2) Problem Lists, (3) Intervention Plans, and (4) Progress Notes. Figure 5-1 illustrates the connections between these component parts of the POFTR and shows how they create cybernetic feedback loops. The organizational structure of the record encourages more explicit documentation of the implicit logic used to arrive at interventions. That is, the logical connections in the structure of the record reflect the implicit conceptual process used by clinicians when they work with families. Given certain initial bits of information (in the data base), a problem is first known through a process of inductive reasoning. Immediately, however, goodness-of-fit feedback (i.e., matching with other data) operates to refine the definition of the problem. Once a problem has been clearly identified, a relevant intervention plan is developed through a process of deductive reasoning. As particular intervention strategies are entertained, their appropriateness for the specific problem is examined. Subsequently, the intervention is applied through the executive process of the therapist's action and reviewed for accuracy of implementation. Finally, the effectiveness of the whole therapeutic endeavor is determined by noting the outcome, which constitutes new data. As indicated in Figure 5-1 the implementation feedback, appropriateness feedback, and goodness-of-fit feedback all eventually lead back to the data base. These feedback loops make it possible for the record to reflect (at least to some extent) the dynamic and evolving nature of the overall assessment and treatment processes.

The POFTR differs from Weed's original POMR in one major way. Several problem lists are developed rather than one. The POMR is a person oriented record and all the patient's individual problems are listed on a single sheet. Consequently, in the POMR, family problems tend to be described in individual terms. In the POFTR there is one summary sheet to list the problems of each individual family member and a second to list problems at various interpersonal system levels. These levels include:

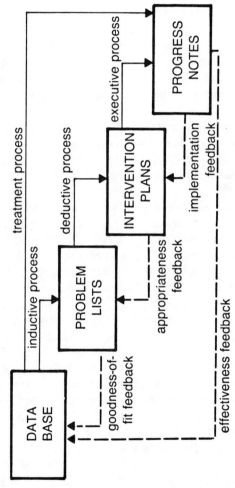

Figure 5-1 Structure of the Problem Oriented Family Therapy Record

- the marital subsystem
- parent-child subsystem
- sibling subsystem
- whole family subsystem
- community–family system
- therapist–family system

This second problem sheet is a very significant addition. The multiplicity of levels on the sheet implicitly encourages the clinician to consider more carefully the particular level at which he or she should define a problem. The choice of intervention is of course heavily influenced by the level at which a problem is defined. Often a core family issue is best described as several problems at multiple levels. Thus a chronic or recurrent family argument may reflect individual, dyadic, triadic, or more complex social problems simultaneously. As more aspects of a problematic issue are considered and understood, a more comprehensive and complex assessment is possible.

The problem lists are placed in a prominent location in the front of the record and thus serve as an easily accessible and succinct current summary of the case. One basic rule when using the problem oriented record is that problems are entered using words or phrases that are most descriptive of the problem as it is currently understood. The use of natural language (rather than technical jargon) is encouraged in order to allow a greater range of descriptive possibilities. A second rule is that multiple problems are entered. No effort is made to arrive at a singular diagnosis. A third rule is that as more and/or better data are obtained, the entries are revised. The use of feedback (as reflected in the logic of the record) automatically activates the revision rule. A fourth rule is that problems are not prioritized in the record. The most important issues raised in a specific session are addressed at that particular time. Finally, considerable attention is paid to how the current issue relates to other problems. Hence a fifth rule is that, when possible, problems are combined and redefined at higher systems levels.

This final rule is very important and requires elaboration. The assessment usually begins with the description of individual problems and then moves toward increasing complexity. Depending on goodness-of-fit, several lower level problems may be combined and integrated into a higher level, more systemic description. This integrative process is strongly encouraged as assessment and therapy progress, because interventions based on higher level problems usually are more efficient in precipitating constructive change. For instance, a husband/father may present as depressed. It may be noted that he has a tendency to withdraw. These behavior patterns may be entered on his individual problem list. Subsequently, the therapist may note that the wife/mother appears to be frustrated and angry much of the time. She has a strong tendency to blame. Provided there is evidence in the temporal sequence of behavioral interaction, her problems may be integrated with his problems and described as a circular pattern of blame-withdrawal in the marriage. The problem is then entered on the problem list at the marital subsystem level. An intervention aimed at changing the interaction pattern in the marriage is liable to have a greater and more lasting impact on the father's initial depression than an intervention which focuses on the father or the mother individually. Later, as more data accumulate, it may become apparent that the children are aligned with the mother and split away from the father. The mother and children may also be deeply involved with her family of origin. The problem then may be redefined as one of unbalanced affiliations in the whole family system. An intervention aimed at altering the overall organization of the whole family is liable to have an even greater impact on the father's initial depression than an intervention that targets only the marital relationship. Thus considerable effort should be devoted to making connections between problems and to develop a more complete systemic understanding by combining and revising the problems on the list.

If after a series of interventions the outcome indicates that there has been no change, it is probable that there is a flaw either in the definition of the problem being targeted or in the logical connections leading to the interventions that were applied. If the latter connections appear sound, the problem itself must be reexamined for goodness-of-fit with the data. Hence the emphasis on continual reassessment.

However, any assessment depends on the quality of data upon which it is based. If information about a family is descriptive and documented with minimal inference, it often may be reinterpreted later and used to support new hypotheses regarding the nature of underlying problems. However if data are to be retained in relatively "raw" descriptive form, then some sort of ad hoc organizational structure is required to know where to locate it in the data base. The family assessment model described below has been devised to provide this structure within the POFTR. The information collected about the family is entered according to type of datum, not according to time of collection (date of data entries) or according to source of entry (whether a student, the therapist, or a supervisor). There is a specific location on each of the data forms for specific types of information. Regardless of when the data are collected or who enters the data on the record, they still end up in the same location. Thus when a problem definition is being revised, a specific datum can easily be retrieved, reviewed, and possibly reinterpreted.

THE FAMILY ASSESSMENT MODEL

Our family assessment model (FAM) is sometimes referred to as the Tripartite Model because it is divided into three major sections: family structure, family functioning, and family development. These three sections are, of course, interrelated but they offer somewhat different perspectives on the family. The family structure section is intended to provide an initial overall gestalt of the family. This includes its internal composition as well as its social and geographical contexts. The family functioning section focuses on here-and-now patterns of interaction in the family, while the developmental section is oriented toward a historical perspective.

The FAM is organized into a hierarchical branching structure. Sections are divided into parts, parts into categories, and categories into specific subheadings or cues. The family structure section includes two major parts: internal structure and external structure. Family functioning in turn is divided into two parts: instrumental functioning and expressive functioning. Family development is also divided into two parts: specific problem development and general family life cycle development. Each of these six parts of the assessment is represented in the record by a specific form. The forms in turn are organized internally in that most are divided into categories that are subdivided for specific bits of data. Figure 5-2 illustrates this overall organizational structure.

The FAM is not intended as a fill-in-the-blanks guide to direct the course of an assessment interview. The therapist's own natural curiosity, his or her emerging hypotheses, interviewing skill, and creativity in devising useful questions should guide the moment-to-moment interaction with the family during the interview. The assessment model is intended rather as a format within which one can organize data (that the therapist has already obtained) after he or she has completed the interview. The

Figure 5-2 Structure of the Family Assessment Model (FAM)

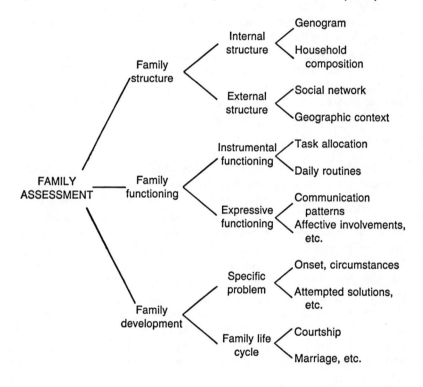

data are entered in the appropriate locations on the relevant forms of the record as the data becomes available.

The internal organization of the FAM is based on a number of implicit conceptual distinctions. Some of these may be relatively arbitrary and reflect the personal preferences of the first author who originally devised the record system and the assessment model. However, the theoretical orientation prevalent in the program at the time the model was developed certainly had a major impact on which distinctions were incorporated (Tomm, 1980). Generally, the model is based on general systems theory as applied to families. However, concepts from cybernetics, communications theory, behaviorism, psychoanalysis, and ethology have been included as well. The following discussion will attempt to clarify some of the major concepts embedded in the model. The two forms comprising each section will be described briefly to provide a flavor of the type of data collected and how it is managed.

STRUCTURAL ASSESSMENT

There are two parts to the structural assessment: internal family structure and external family structure. The internal–external distinction implies that a boundary exists between the inside and the outside of the family. This boundary may be more or less distinct and more or less stable, depending on the family and its context. External family structure refers to the nature of connections across a hypothetical family boundary. Internal structure refers to the constellation of family membership within the boundary. However, the delineation of a family boundary is much more difficult than one might suspect. It requires a precise definition of the family. This is particularly difficult when there have been multiple marriages and offspring from various sexual unions. In practice we use two pragmatic definitions: (1) the present composition of the household and (2) a genogram of all (past and present) conjugal and filial ties. The relevant data from both definitions are summarized in the record on a single diagram of the family genogram with a line drawn around all those on the genogram who live in the current household. A few basic rules have been devised to standardize the method of drawing genograms (squares represent males, circles females, older siblings on the left, etc.) so that a glance at the family diagram gives the therapist or supervisor an immediate gestalt of the family under consideration. Figure 5-3 illustrates how the standardized format and notations convey a great deal of orienting information accurately and quickly.

Figure 5-3 Sample Genogram

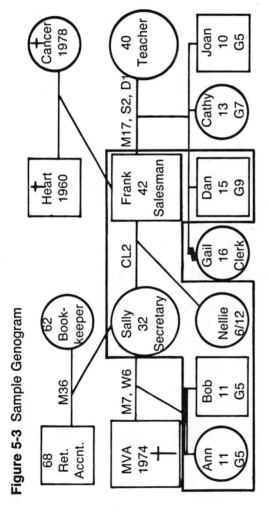

Note: Included in the current household is Sally (who was married 7 years, then widowed 6), her twins, Ann and Bob (age 11 in Grade 5), Frank, (her common-law-husband of 2 years), Nellie (their daughter, 6 months), and Dan (Frank's 15-year-old son of a previous marriage). Frank has three other children, Gail, 16 (who was adopted), Cathy, 13, and Joan, 10. His ex-wife is a teacher and both his parents are deceased. Sally's parents are still alive and have been married 36 years. Her first husband was killed in a motor vehicle accident in 1974.

The external family structure part of the record includes data regarding geographic location and mobility, socioeconomic status, institutional involvements, (e.g., employment, school, medicine, law), and social network contacts (e.g., extended family, friends, neighbors). Most of this information is obtained in a three-page questionnaire completed by the family prior to the first interview. One major disadvantage in obtaining information by questionnaire is that the relative importance of specific bits of data is difficult to determine. When obtaining information through interviewing, relevance is conveyed in the choice of words, tone of voice, and nonverbal responses (of the speaker and of other family members). This additional information concerning current significance of data actually forms part of our functional assessment. The structural assessment is only intended to provide an initial gestalt or overview of the family unit and its context. It might be helpful to point out here that concepts associated with Minuchin's structural assessment (1974)—for instance, internal affiliations and boundaries—are included as part of our functional assessment.

FUNCTIONAL ASSESSMENT

The functional assessment focuses on current patterns of behavior. It is concerned with the details of how family members actually behave in their day to day activities and particularly in relation to one another. Functional family assessment is divided into instrumental and expressive parts. The instrumental assessment focuses on the routine activities of daily living with respect to fulfilling physical needs, maintaining the household, attending work or school, etc. Expressive family functioning focuses on the patterns of interpersonal relationships. The basic distinction here is that behaviors may be regarded as physical events (instrumental functioning) or as communicative events (expressive functioning). This section of the FAM is distinguished from the development section in its being oriented toward a cross-sectional, here-and-now time perspective.

The form used to document instrumental data is organized to reflect the sequences of a typical day from waking and breakfast routines to bedtime and night routines. There are separate columns on the form for weekday and weekend patterns. While this part of the record is seldom used, some of the instrumental data (e.g., sleeping arrangements) often has significant ramifications for patterns of expressive functioning. A concrete picture of actual behaviors and physical sequences in the household provides a solid base for making inferences about communicative meaning. Thus we encourage beginning students (and experienced therapists when they are stuck) to be comprehensive in collecting instrumental data and to document them in a descriptive manner that allows for reinterpretation later.

The expressive family functioning form is probably the most useful component of the FAM (next to the genogram). There are nine major categories on the form, which presents a reworked and expanded version of the Family Categories Schema devised by Epstein, Segal, and Rakoff (1968). These categories are basic interaction, affective communication, verbal communication, problem solving, roles, behavior controls, family beliefs and goals, affective involvement and therapist–family system. Each category is subdivided into several minor headings or cues for the precise location of specific information. Exhibit 5-1 is a reproduction of the top portion of the Expressive Family Functioning form, which shows 12 cues in the category of basic interaction and 9 in affective communication.

We feel that the cueing system adds to the usefulness of the record. It serves as an aid to recall and as an implicit suggestion for further enquiry. When entering data in the category of affective communication the therapist may be stimulated to consider and reflect on a wider range of affects than he or she was consciously aware of during the interview. Imagine a therapist completing his or her records after a session dominated by anger and contempt. There may have been brief expressions of warmth and affection that were noticed preconsciously but were not attended to during the interview. The cue in the record may trigger the therapist's recall and the information then becomes available in his or her consciousness for more careful analysis of covert affiliations. Without the cue the affectionate signals could easily be entirely overlooked and quickly forgotten. Further, if the therapist could not recall any expressions of anxiety or fear, the cue may stimulate him or her to consider enquiring about possible fears or catastrophic expectations in the next session.

As indicated in Exhibit 5-1, the data on the Expressive Family Functioning form is further differentiated as being "reported by family or others" (subjective) or being "observed by therapist" (objective). This is a very useful distinction and hence separate columns are provided for each type of datum. What people say about how they relate to others is often not necessarily what neutral observers see them do. In fact, in order

Exhibit 5-1 Expressive Family Functioning Form

EXPRESSIVE FAMILY FUNCTIONING

The focus for data on this form is here and now, current family functioning in the affective-relational sense. Differentiate carefully between direct observational evidence and hearsay evidence reported by family members and/or others. Use standard notations where relevant: M-Mother, etc.

FAMILY NAME_____ CASE #_____ DATE STARTED_____

	Observed by Therapist	Reported by Family or Others
1. BASIC INTERACTION		
1.1 time in proximity		
1.2 proxemics (spacing)		
1.3 initiators/reactors		
1.4 interruptions		
1.5 kinesic activity		
1.6 physical contact		
1.7 facial expressiveness		
1.8 eye contact		
1.9 relative talk time		
1.10 direction/partitioning		
1.11 rate and rhythm of speech		
1.12 tonality of speech		
2. AFFECTIVE COMMUNICATION		
2.1 interest/attention		
2.2 happiness/excitement		
2.3 affection/warmth		
2.4 disappointment/sadness		
2.5 anxiety/fear		
2.6 shame/guilt		
2.7 disgust/contempt		
2.8 frustration/covert anger		
2.9 overt anger/rage		
3. VERBAL COMMUNICATION		
3.1 direct/displaced		
3.2 clear/masked/distorted		

to continue their patterns of interaction the system may "require" that some family members not be consciously aware of certain behaviors or interaction patterns. A mother complaining that a child is too withdrawn and quiet is unlikely to note that she regularly interrupts and speaks for the child. The separation of data into columns according to source in this part of the record tends to highlight such discrepancies. These in turn may become an additional source of important information about the functioning of the system.

Any particular communicative behavior or event can be documented with a varying degree of precision and inference. Data entries at lower levels of abstraction tend to be descriptive and reflect observable behaviors, while entries at higher levels of abstraction tend to be inferential and reflect speculative patterns. Descriptive details are much less useful than inferential patterns when it comes to developing a comprehensive understanding of the functioning of the whole family as a system. On the other hand, while inferential data provide a larger view, precision and accuracy may be lost. For example, a child's response to questions may be recorded as "occasionally speaks in a low monotone voice, turns head and eyes to the ceiling." This is low abstraction data; no inferences are made. On the other hand, this same behavior could be recorded as "he's disinterested." The latter entry may be more economical but represents an inference. It is an interpretation of the observed behaviors. As more information is generated and alternative hypotheses are entertained, it may be useful to reinterpret earlier data. The child's response style may have been intended to show disdain and contempt or alternatively it may have been due to epileptiform activity. Such reinterpretation is possible with low level descriptive data but not with more abstract inferential data. Both types of data may be entered on the expressive functioning form. In general, the nine categories on the form have been arranged to follow an order of increasing inference, that is, toward higher levels of abstraction. Basic interaction (category 1) includes relative talk time and eye contact, which are readily observable, while affective involvements (category 8) are inferred from general patterns of behavior. At these points of high inference the connections to the problem list are very close.

DEVELOPMENTAL ASSESSMENT

There are two parts to this section of the assessment model. Both emphasize a longitudinal time perspective, including past, present, and anticipated events. One part focuses on the data generated from an enquiry into the nature and development of a specific problem. Such data are entered on the Detailed Problem Development form, which is always used to collate information about the presenting problem and its evolution. The form may also be used to bring together, in one location, data regarding any other problem entered on the problem list. The other part of the developmental assessment entails the documentation of major events (normative and accidental) that the family has experienced as it moved through its life cycle. The basic distinction here is between the emerging problem and its evolving context. For systems-oriented theorists who tend to see the problem as a function of its context, this distinction in the record may seem more problematic than useful. However, having a separate form to systematically record data on the family life cycle does serve to add weight to the importance of the data. The evolutionary nature of the context of the problem is overlooked all too often.

The developmental assessment forms also are organized internally into categories, each with its subheadings or cues. The major categories on the problem development form are: initial appearance, problem progression, attempts to rectify, present status, decision to seek therapy, and future goals. There are also separate columns for "internal perceptions" (of family members) and for "external perceptions" (of the school, doctor, police, etc.) of the problem and related events. While therapists usually collect data about the presenting problem in a systematic fashion during the beginning of the first interview, information relevant to the family life cycle usually emerges spontaneously and piecemeal over the course of therapy. Regardless of how and when the information is obtained, family life cycle data is organized in a chronological framework and kept in its appropriate location in the file. The categories on the family development form reflect the progressive stages of an idealized family life cycle: courtship, marriage, expansion, early child rearing, late child rearing, departure of the children, and integration. The choice of these seven stages is relatively arbitrary (various developmental theorists use from 2 to 24 stages). A special Alternative Family Development form was devised with the assistance of one of our students for use with single parent and/or blended families.

Like Erikson's eight ages of man (1950), each family life cycle stage is associated with critical development tasks and transitions. Courtship entails the selection of a compatible mate and making a commitment that implies an attenuation of other peer relationships. Marriage involves a reduction of each spouse's involvement with their families of origin and a consolidation of primary loyalties toward the marital partner. The notorious in-law problems are often a result of the failure to make this critical transition. Expansion involves the birth of children and requires each family member to allow space for the new child in the family. This task must be accomplished by developing new bonds with the child while creatively realigning marital and other commitments. Difficulties in accomplishing this task may result in a husband experiencing displacement and competition with the child for the wife/mother's attention. In preparation for departure of the children, the parents must be able to gradually relinquish control as adolescent children become more autonomous. When the children actually leave, the couple must again realign their marriage to adjust to the change in family structure. There are many ways in which this developmental process may go awry. Collecting family life cycle data in one location in the record makes it easier to generate a comprehensive overview. This in turn helps the therapist understand the idiosyncrasies of each family's development and how it may have contributed to the emergence of the presenting problem. Juxtaposing the Detailed Problem Development and Family Development forms in the record enhances the probability that the therapist will make conceptual connections between "pathological" interaction patterns and "normal" family developmental tasks. As a result of completing the developmental assessment, the problem definition may be revised. Consequently, a different type of intervention may be deduced and applied.

DISCUSSION

As with any model the assessment approach outlined has certain disadvantages and limitations. For instance, the branches in the record, when taken to the "bottom" of the hierarchical structure, are very numerous. It appears as if an extraordinary amount of detail is being expected. Record keeping would become a major burden if the therapist responded to every cue and entered data under every subheading. The record is not intended to be used in this manner. Because a location exists for a certain type of datum does not mean that something needs to be entered in that location. On the contrary, when a certain datum exists, it merely has a specific location in which to be entered. However, the comprehensiveness of the model does pose difficulty for therapists who tend to be obsessive in their recording habits. On the other hand, this very same characteristic of the record is useful for those therapists who tend to be rather loose and undisciplined in their recording and conceptualizing.

A more serious disadvantage is that the conceptual distinctions made in constructing the model are now part of it. These distinctions may not be the most useful ones in facilitating heuristic connections in the mind of the therapist. As de Shazer (1982) points out, certain distinctions are not useful and may in fact lead to muddled thinking. At this stage it is difficult to know which distinctions may be inadvertently confusing and which are genuinely clarifying. One thing is certain, however: distinctions are being made. To build a model to organize data for easy retrieval implies that the categories must remain stable. Indeed, because of this stability the assessment model takes on some of the same limitations as family diagnosis discussed earlier. However, because most of the fixed distinctions occur at lower levels of abstraction they have less encompassing effects.

It is important to emphasize that the assessment process described here is post hoc, that is, it takes place following the interview with the family. What we have described is not how to elicit data from families but how to use it once it has been obtained. We are fully aware of the fact that the quality of any post hoc analysis is entirely dependent on the nature and quality of data on which it is based. Thus we believe that what transpires between the family and the therapist in the actual interview is far more important. The skills involved in eliciting the most useful information from families in the most efficient manner is a very important subject that has not been addressed in this article. The first author has commented on two quite different approaches to eliciting information during the interview in separate papers (Tomm, 1982; Tomm & Wright, 1979). The family assessment method described here is proposed as an adjunct to, not a substitute for, effective interviewing skills.

All facets of our record system have not been described in this article. For instance, there are other sections to the data base in addition to the FAM. Specific forms are provided for mental status and developmental assessment of individual adults and children. A program contact sheet maintains a chronological record of all contacts (interviews, other face to face meetings, telephone calls, and letters) with the family or relevant others (referral source, relatives, etc.). Some "guide notes" have also been prepared to explain the use of forms, define rules for drawing genograms, elaborate on the meaning of specific cues, etc. A complete set of forms in the POFTR may be obtained by writing the authors.

Our experience in using this record system has been that it is not only an aid to the therapist in his or her assessment and treatment of families but that it is also an effective teaching tool. When students are asked to complete the record after an interview, they are placed in a position to externalize their conceptualization of the case. Thus on reviewing their documentation the supervisor is able to be much more specific in identifying and commenting on interview events or family issues that he or she interprets differently. The process of comparing specific perceptions and inferences greatly facilitates the development of perceptual and conceptual skills. Furthermore, a quick review of the problems entered in the problem list reveals the amount of effort and skill that the student (or therapist) has put into formulating problems. If the entries are predominantly at the individual level, the student clearly needs assistance in conceptualizing at more complex interpersonal systems levels. During the seven years that this record system has been used in the Calgary program, it has greatly facilitated the accuracy and effectiveness of clinical communication among our staff and students. Most significantly, however, it has undoubtedly contributed to the quality of our work with families.

REFERENCES

Benjamin, L.S. Structural analysis of social behavior. *Psychological Review*, 1974, *81*(5), 392–425.

Broderick, C.B., & Schroder, S.S. The history of professional marriage and family therapy. In A.S. Gurman & D.P. Kniskern (Eds.), *Handbook of family therapy.* New York: Brunner Mazel, 1981.

Cuber, J.F., & Harroff, P.B., *The significant Americans: A study of sexual behavior among the affluent.* New York: Appleton Century, 1965.

de Shazer, S. Some conceptual distinctions are more useful than others. *Family Process*, 1982, *21*(1), 71–84.

Dorland's Illustrated *Medical Dictionary* (24th Ed.). Philadelphia: Saunders, 1965.

Epstein, N.B., Segal, J.J., & Rakoff, V. Family categories schema. Unpublished manuscript. Montreal: Jewish General Hospital, 1968.

Erikson, E. *Childhood and society.* New York: Norton, 1950.

Fisher, L. On the classification of families. *Archives of General Psychiatry*, 1977, *34*, 424–433.

Hoffman, L. *Foundations of family therapy.* New York: Basic, 1980.

Minuchin, S. *Families and family therapy.* Cambridge, Mass.: Harvard, 1974.

Olson, D., Sprenkle, D., & Russell, C. Circumplex model of marital and family systems:

1. Cohesion and adaptability dimensions, family types and clinical applications. *Family Process*, 1979, *18*(1), 3–28.

Tomm, K.M. Towards a cybernetic-systems approach to family therapy at the University of Calgary. In D.S. Freeman (Ed.), *Perspectives on family therapy*. Vancouver: Butterworth, 1980.

Tomm, K.M. The Milan Approach to family therapy: A tentative report. In D. Freeman & B. Trute (Eds.), *Treating families with special needs*. Ottawa: Canadian Association of Social Workers, 1982.

Tomm, K.M., & Wright, L.M. Training in family therapy: Perceptual, conceptual, and executive skills. *Family Process*, 1979, *28*(3), 227–250.

Weed, L.L. Medical records, medical education and patient care: The problem oriented record as basic tool. Cleveland: Case Western Reserve University, 1970.

6. Diagnosing = Researching + Doing Therapy

Steve de Shazer
Director
Brief Family Therapy Center
Milwaukee, Wisconsin

Six

THE WORD *DIAGNOSIS* COMES FROM TWO GREEK WORDS THAT together mean "to determine between." The notion of classification follows. Frequently, the term is used to describe the process of determining, by examination, the nature and circumstances of a diseased condition, and the decision reached from such an examination. In medicine and therapy, this is held to be a scientific determination, a description that classifies something precisely.

But of more interest to the family therapist, and therapists interested in systems, are the meanings of the second half of the word: *gnosis*. This term generally means "knowledge" and is frequently used to refer to "special or mystical knowledge." For instance, during the early Christian era, a *gnostic* was one who knew God in a special, mystical way. Based on the Greek roots of the word, *diagnosis* can be seen to have something to do with epistemology: the branch of art, science, and philosophy that is concerned with how we know, think, and decide.

Over the years since the start of family therapy there have been frequent calls for developing a new nosology, one not based on the "disease" of one individual member of the family system but based on the "dis-ease" of the family system. Of course, early efforts in this direction attempted to establish the relationship(s) between the individual "disease" and the family's "dis-ease." That is, the pioneers attempted to develop a classification that had a one to one relationship between the individual symptom and some particular "type" or "structure" of family. There were attempts to describe the family of the schizophrenic, the family of the ulcerative colitis patient, the family of the delinquent. And, although there may be some differences between these "types" of families, clinically speaking therapy seems to follow other patterns which make all of these "types" not quite relevant from a clinical viewpoint.

In previous papers (1978, 1979) the author attempted to develop what might be described as a nosology based on the structural balance of families. It had little or nothing to do with the individual "dis-ease" or symptom. For that matter, no specific balance structure was seen as related to anything other than the type of interactional patterns between, and among, the family members. That is, the nosology was mathematical and interactional rather than pathological. The balance theoretical model of the family interaction patterns also attempted to give some rigor to the notion of *homeostatic mechanisms,* which can be seen to be what keeps the family system within the homeostatic constraints. The mapping tools of this model enabled the observer to describe the homeostatic mechanisms of the interpersonal relationships in such a way that a step-by-step approach to the specific family's therapy could be developed. However, this model had more to do with how we *know family systems* than how we *know what is going on in family therapy.* The model had more to do with understanding homeostatic stability than with the processes of changing, which is the business of therapy.

The balance theoretical model, like most family therapy models, failed to make a clear distinction between *the study of the family as a system* and *the study of family therapy as a system.* Although guidelines for promoting change were an integral part of the model, it did not have enough to say about the ecosystemic nature of the family therapy situation. That is, although the therapist's relationship to the family system was sketched, it was not seen as crucial to the understanding of the therapy situation. With this tool, the therapist could *know* a lot about a specific family but he could *not know* about the ecosystemic relationship between the therapist subsystem and the family subsystem. Thus the epistemological error was perpetuated which kept the therapist as an observer somehow separate from the family system. The model did not explicitly deal with the impact of the observer upon the observed and therefore the methodological boundary was drawn around the family as a system rather than around the larger therapy situation as a system.

HOW SYSTEMS KNOW

Once we make a clear distinction between the study of the family as a system and the study of family therapy as a system, the question "How do systems know?'' becomes central to the process of diagnosing. The therapist is seen as one subsystem while the family is seen as another subsystem of the therapeutic suprasystem. Maruyama (1977) describes the way systems know as "poly-ocular" or as a "cross-subjective" way of knowing. This way of knowing is similar to the way in which the two eyes cooperate in the development of depth perception. The right eye sees an object from a particular point of view while the left eye sees the same object from a slightly different point of view, and the *bonus* of depth perception develops because of the difference between the two points of view. This difference enables us to compute a dimension that is invisible to either eye alone. Binocular vision allows us to see three-dimensionally because of the difference between the two images.

In the therapy situation the family describes (and shows) their view of the problem or "dis-ease" which brings them to therapy. They describe this situation from a certain, particular point of view (the "family's eye view"). While this is going on, the therapist describes the same situation (to himself or herself at least) from a different point of view (the "therapist's eye view"). Thus the therapist *knows* the family situation both from his point of view and from the family's point of view as they report it. From the differences between these points of view, the therapist is able to develop a *bonus* which leads to an intervention which can prompt changing in the family subsystem and the therapist subsystem. The poly-ocular way in which systems know is related to Bateson's notion that "ideas" (bonuses) develop from having two or more descriptions of the same process or sequence that are coded or collected differently (Bateson, 1979). That is, a relationship develops between the two descriptions derived from different points of view. This relationship results in a view from a different angle or a bonus, similar to the bonus of depth perception.

In very simple terms, the family can be seen as describing their situation from a *negative* point of view (otherwise there would be no "dis-ease") and the therapist can develop a *positive* point of view in his hypothesis that will guarantee a different angle. For example, if a couple sees their fights as driving them apart, the therapist might see these same fights as holding them together (if for no other reason than the fights have not yet driven them apart). If the therapist hypothesizes that the fights hold the couple together, then his intervention is going to be different from the couple's attempts to solve the problem. Obviously, the intervention might go so far as describing to the couple the idea that their fights hold them together and suggesting they continue to fight at least until "new glue" can be invented.

Diagnosing as a process can be seen to start with the family's description and the therapist's description of the same situation. From the juxtaposition of these two descriptions, a bonus develops that prompts the intervention, and which in turn is designed to prompt some sort of changing in the family subsystem, and therefore in the therapeutic suprasystem. As Haley (1963) might have said, the couple either stops fighting, or they now fight because the therapist told them to (since it holds them together) rather than because they cannot help it. Either of these outcomes is a report on the relationships in the therapeutic suprasystem. (Of course fighting or not fighting are not the only possible outcomes.) Any outcome reported by the family not only defines their relationship with the therapist, but it also calls for the therapist to change his or her response. If, for instance, the couple is no longer fighting, then the therapist *knows* something about the suprasystemic relationship he or she did not know before. In the circumstances, it would be a diagnosing error to still treat the couple as having a problem with fighting. Instead, the therapist needs to develop another hypothesis about how to keep the couple continuing to be nonfighters. If the couple is optimistic about the fights being over, the therapist might predict a relapse. Or, if the couple is skeptical about the duration of peace, the therapist might prescribe a preventative fight. In any case, the choice of intervention depends on the suprasystemic relationships. However, if the couple is still fighting, the therapist *knows* something different about the suprasystemic relationship. He might hypothesize, in this situation, that this couple will follow therapeutic directives. And thus a hypothesis might be developed that leads to further instructions for continued fights but in different ways or circumstances.

Diagnosing is thus a process that evolves in this way:

1. the family's description
2. the therapist's description
3. the intervention
4. the family's reported response to that intervention
5. the therapist's response to the family's response: another intervention

And then, in recursive fashion, this process repeats. In the next session the family will describe their response from a certain angle and the therapist will describe (to himself at least) that response from his point of view, and the intervention will be based on that juxtaposition of points of view.

Thus any sort of nosology useful for diagnosing in family therapy needs to keep in mind the changing nature of the process of therapy and the development of the relationships in the therapeutic suprasystem. That is, a nosology that freezes action and describes either just the family as a system or the individual "dis-ease" is not built on the way systems *know* and behave. The nosology, if it can be still called by that name, must instead describe the ebb and flow of the developing patterns and must be designed to take into account the responsive behaviors of both the family subsystem and the therapist subsystem: the behavior of the therapeutic suprasystem.

THE DECISION TREE

With the concept of the therapeutic process described above, any response the family makes to an intervention given them by the therapist is defined as "cooperating" (de Shazer, 1982) or as responsive behavior.

> . . . any of the possibilities constitute responsive behavior. Thus a situation is created in which the subject can express his resistance in a constructive, cooperative fashion; manifestation of resistance by a subject is best utilized by developing a situation in which resistance serves a purpose. (Erickson, cited in Haley, 1967, p. 20)

Although "resistance" may be a poor metaphor for an ecosystemic therapy (de Shazer, 1982), the point is well taken. Each response by a family is seen as cooperating or responsive behavior that further defines the therapeutic relationship.

It is not just a simple matter of "either the family reports a response in the direction of change or they do not." The therapy relationship is more complex than a simple "either/or" description permits. Many therapeutic interventions include tasks or homework assignments designed to promote changing. Additionally, response reports from the family about task performance can be the therapist's best guide to the family's definition of that relationship and for defining the therapeutic relationship.

For instance, if the therapist gives the family a task, the response report is likely to fall into one of these five categories, all responsive behaviors:

1. the family might report straightforward performance of a concrete task
2. the family might report performing a modification of the concrete task
3. the family might report doing the opposite of the behaviors called for by the concrete task
4. the family might give a report that is so vague that the therapist is perplexed by the report
5. the family might report not having done the concrete task.

Each of these response reports is a communication about the relationship between the component subsystems. Each response report demonstrates the family's unique manner of cooperating with the therapist subsystem and requires a response from the therapist (an intervention) that is based on the knowledge gained from the previous interactions.

THERAPIST RESPONSES

Based on the new knowledge gained through the response report, the therapist needs to design the next intervention. Each of the five categories of response report calls for a type of intervention that makes use of the knowledge gained in order to promote changing.

If the therapist gives the family the concrete task of counting the number of times the child is observed to suck his thumb, and the family accepts the task, the family's response report can fall into any of the five (above) categories, and this helps to define the next intervention:

1. If the family reports straightforward performance, this indicates that their relationship with the therapist includes doing what the therapist told them to do. Therefore, the next intervention can be another straightforward task.

2. If the family reports counting on only two or three of the days between sessions, this indicates that their relationship with the therapist includes their modifying the directives he gave them. Therefore, the therapist can continue cooperating by giving the family a task that is easily modifiable. For instance, the therapist might tell the family to randomly do something different at various odd times when they catch the child sucking his thumb.

3. If the family reports not counting because they never caught tne child sucking his thumb, this can be seen as an "opposite" response. The therapist can continue cooperating by giving the family an intervention which calls for, or allows for, an opposite response. For instance, the therapist might tell the child to start sucking his thumb in an obvious manner so that the parents can test their observation skills.

4. If the family's report is so vague that the therapist cannot have any clear idea of frequency or task performance, then this is a clear message about the family's manner of cooperating. If the therapist receives this message as a responsive message, then he can continue cooperating with the family's manner of cooperating by giving them a vague task. Another concrete task at this point can be seen as oppositional and might destroy the therapeutic relationship. For instance, the therapist might tell the family a story about how some other similar family with a thumb sucker solved their problem without ever indicating directly that the family should do anything specific.

5. If the family's response report indicates that they did not do the task, even this response can be defined as cooperative. The therapist can then best continue cooperating by not giving a concrete task. For instance, the therapist might apologize for having given the family the wrong task in the previous session and congratulate them for not having done the task that they intuitively knew could only make things worse.

Although these are not the only responses the therapist might appropriately make, these interventions nonetheless demonstrate how the knowledge gained from the previous intervention can be utilized. In subsequent sessions, the family's response report might switch categories, and the therapist can best continue cooperating by following along and also switching the type of intervention.

Of course each intervention, regardless of type, must be constructed from the therapist's eye view of the situation in order to create the bonus. Otherwise the family will not receive the news of difference and there will not be the bonus of therapy: changing.

CONCLUSION

The process of diagnosing can be seen as an epistemological activity aimed at using the "gnosis" part of the word: *a special way of knowing.*

As a research activity, diagnosing calls for the building of a hypothesis and then testing out this hypothesis by giving tasks or interventions used as a probe into the suprasystemic relationship. From the family system's reported response to this probe, the therapist gains new knowledge and therefore refines the hypothesis or builds a new hypothesis that can be tested out with the subsequent interventions. Therefore each therapy session becomes an "experiment" with the outcome measured in the following session.

Of course this research must be seen as going somewhere, and therefore the activity can also be called "doing therapy." Since the goal of therapy is changing, it is important for the family to have defined how they will know when the problem is solved. Otherwise neither family nor therapist can know the effectiveness of their work.

This three-faced activity, diagnosing = researching + doing therapy, is based on "ecosystemic gnosis," a special way in which systems know. Although the formula retains a somewhat linear form, each of these activities (diagnosing, researching, and doing therapy) is simultaneous and recursive. Each attempts to define and artificially separate different aspects of the same activity. Each, separately and together, in some way answers the epistemological question: How do we, as part of a therapeutic suprasystem or ecosystem, know?

REFERENCES

Bateson, G. *Mind and nature: A necessary unity.* New York: Dutton, 1979.

de Shazer, S. Brief therapy with couples. *International Journal of Family Counseling,* 1978, *6*, 17–30.

de Shazer, S. Brief therapy with families. *American Journal of Family Therapy,* 1979, *7*, 83–95.

de Shazer, S. *Patterns of brief family therapy: An ecosystemic approach.* New York: Guilford Press, 1982.

Haley, J. *Strategies of psychotherapy.* New York: Grune & Stratton, 1963.

Haley, J. (Ed.). *Advanced techniques of hypnosis and therapy: Selected papers of Milton H. Erickson, M.D.* New York: Grune & Stratton, 1967.

Maruyama, M. Heterogenistics: An epistemological restructuring of biological and social sciences. *Cybernetica,* 1977, *20*, 69–86.

7. The Beginning Family Therapist and Dilemmas in Diagnosis

George S. Greenberg, D.S.W.
Director
Family Therapy Institute of Greater New Orleans, Inc.
Assistant Clinical Professor of Psychiatry
Louisiana State University Medical School
New Orleans, Louisiana

Seven

THE NOVICE TO FAMILY THERAPY IS FOR THE MOST PART FACED with the same types of struggles and difficulties as the novice being introduced to individual psychotherapy. The novice is searching for a workable formula or set of ideas (a viewpoint) that can be drawn upon as a coherent organized frame of reference with which to make sense and order out of the phenomena that occur in the "treatment or evaluative" therapy sessions.

A basic criterion of all sound therapeutic activity is that the professional should have at least one highly organized theory pertaining to human problems. This theoretical base must include notions regarding:

- human nature
- views on how to judge or measure function and dysfunction
- the location of problems or symptoms
- the focus of therapeutic activity
- how to modify dysfunction

Thus, if treatment is to have any direct relationship to what the therapist identifies in the assessment, or in an evaluation leading to diagnosis, it must also have a direct correlation with the therapist's theoretical understanding.

If, for example, the therapist utilizes the corpus of therapy theory and intervention techniques classically identified as a psychoanalytic or psychodynamic orientation, then the focus of diagnosis will correlate to a host of concepts related to processes within the individual, structural and topological ideas that are used to explain dysfunction, and notions of change pertaining to self-awareness, and so forth. Or, one can take an Adlerian viewpoint or even an orthodox Jungian approach providing a firm grounding in the particular and specific theoretical viewpoints.

Without a fundamental theoretical basis that is integrated and institutionalized the therapist can do nothing except respond to the patient's presentations. In effect, one is left to buy time while waiting to discover or to make sense and order out of what is going on.

Additionally, when observing family therapists who have stature in the field, the trainee recognizes that while they are extremely adept at doing assessments they often do not precisely talk or write about how they do assessments, nor do they spell out exactly what they look for. Instead, they tend to speak at a higher level of abstraction, enunciating an overview depicting what they got out of the assessment and how they worked with the family.

The student is thus left with the little bits and pieces of what the master identified that emerged out of the teacher's wide theoretical frame. But without knowledge of the fundamental concepts and a wider gestalt, the student is lost. If not lost, the novice is often quick to oversimplify the processes and further abstract these bits and pieces, arriving at such conclusions as "all the family therapist does is to:

- paradox someone
- create a structural shift
- clear up communication
- block a metaphor
- detriangulate
- and so forth."

At this juncture, the student's "bird's-eye view" often leads to a belief that good family therapy begs diagnosis and strictly tests what bag of techniques can be imposed on the interviewees to gain exciting and interesting effects. If such a viewpoint is not corrected, the therapist goes forth with a dangerously limited set of ideas about family therapy. If this therapist somehow manages to stay in the family therapy arena and, worse, finds a teaching position, the next generation of students will be influenced to mislabel family treatment as a cook-book approach to psychotherapy.

Obviously, the student cannot have a substantive theoretical base grounded in experience. However, a preponderance of training programs for psychotherapists are organized around classical sequences in human growth and development and courses in individual psychopathology. If they exist, courses in the sociology of the family and family therapy generally are left for the latter part of the training sequence. Consequently while the trainee's view of individual functioning and dysfunction is limited in scope, it is often seen by the trainee as expertise, in contrast to the trainee's infinitesimal or nonexistent view of a family perspective. And even if it is not viewed as expertise, it is still used as a firmer basis of theoretical bias by which to view individuals—albeit individuals in families.

Furthermore, when students with classical training are exposed to a family therapy perspective, they are not only not grounded in an individual orientation and the functional premises that viewpoint represents, but frequently in reaching over to a second framework (like family therapy) they follow the same path of borrowing concrete bits and pieces from it.

Here novices to family treatment are faced with another dilemma— unable to integrate concepts from family therapy into a classical analytic perspective, they find that they cannot integrate the fundamental concepts that make up the arena identified under the umbrella term, *family therapy*. This problem is exacerbated by the teacher of family therapy who zealously introduces case materials and foregoes a sound didactic examination of the history and development of family perspectives, and does not adequately clarify for the trainee that family treatment, like individual treatment, comprises a variety of theoretical constructions, therefore making it clear that a number of various frameworks exist, that in and of themselves have not been integrated.

Regrettably, a great number of training programs and courses in family theory are presented in a manner that leaves the students to sift through a potpourri of family literature and to ferret out for themselves basic concepts, including:

- Bowen's *triangulation* (1978, p. 306)
- Bateson and Jackson's *double bind* (Bateson, Jackson, Haley, & Weakland, 1956; Sluzki & Ransom, 1976; Watzlawick, Beavin, & Jackson, 1967; Watzlawick & Weakland, 1977, pp. 208-291)
- Satir, Watzlawick, and Haley's *meta communication* (Haley, 1976, pp. 88, 218, 220; Satir, 1967; Watzlawick, Beavin, & Jackson, 1967, pp. 52-53, 179-183, 260-261)
- Ferreira's *family myths* (1963, 1967)

Here there is an implicit if not explicit suggestion that the basis of proper family diagnosis is to be found within such a shopping list of concepts. In effect, such a spate of ideas is nothing more than a "Tower of Babel" approach, and can only lead to confusion. Typically, the resulting confusion is temporarily put to rest by the teacher of family therapy with a simple but incorrect explanation that goes, "Good family therapists are eclectic, and eclecticism suggests you borrow concepts from various frameworks and utilize them . . ." So now the student has a new rationale and myth to help explain away or beg the problems of incongruency of viewpoints within the family therapy arena.

Obviously such fallacious explanations can only confound matters, because a potpourri of nonintegrated constructs defies a systematic description and understanding of any therapeutic modality. Furthermore, it makes it difficult to make sense and order out of a set of phenomena, which is not only the basis of all diagnosis, but also what diagnosis is itself about.

The tasks of (1) trying to integrate family therapy concepts with classical individually focused viewpoints (that, even if desirable, has yet to be accomplished by the leaders in the field) and (2) attempting to integrate one family therapy viewpoint or framework with another (e.g., Bowen's family systems, 1978, with Watzlawick's interactional view, 1977) might be recognized as an exercise in futility if the novice had a richer introduction to the historical development of psychodynamic or analytic therapies and hence an awareness of the fundamental differences between, say, orthodox Freudian and neo-Freudian positions. But even when there is a clearer recognition of the fundamental differences in premises and of the nuances of emphasis in clinical application of various theoretical positions, there still exists a tendency among trainees who have first been introduced to classical frameworks to view them as making up a consistent coherent supra-theory, even if the trainees were only exposed to Freud, Horney, and Kohut.

Further, the novices who are not caught up in the myth that classical theories make up a coherent integrated body of thought may develop an almost mystical sense that an integrated coherent historical framework exists. This is frequently based on the assumption that because there is a relatively longer and reified history in the development of analytic views, that this by necessity must mean theoretical continuity and consistency.

The student is sometimes unable to see that the classical perspective has within it a number of relatively coherent theoretical sets—Freudian and Jungian, for instance—and he or she may not be aware that family therapy theory also has a number of coherent organized viewpoints, for example:

- structural (Minuchin, 1974; Minuchin & Fishman, 1981)
- strategic (Haley, 1976, 1980; Madanes, 1981)
- interactional (Bodin, 1981; Greenberg, 1977, 1980; Sluzki & Ransom, 1976; Weakland, Fisch, Watzlawick, & Bodin, 1974)

Armed with the belief that classical formats offer a unified coherent theoretical perspective, the student usually in exasperation now takes an interesting turn. He or she reaches for the historically reified classical material in the form of a taxonomy of disease entities—a psychiatric nosology—and presents colleagues and teachers with a copy of the *Diagnostic and Statistical Manual of Mental Disorders, DSM-III* (APA, 1980). The student may also point out that little is said about families in this "Bible of diagnoses."

This is usually a way of challenging the efficacy of family theory while suggesting that a taxonomy of disease entities is the basis for all good diagnosis. What the student is appropriately recognizing is that there are no widely accepted nosologies in family therapy. To presume, however, that if there were, it would lead to an understanding of individual or family dynamics without a basis of theory (let alone practice) in dealing with people is a gross error.

The attempt to utilize a nosology is an important step in the development of the family therapist or any other therapist for that matter. It is also a pivotal point around which the teacher can begin to clarify the basic premises of a therapeutic perspective. For the opportunity is now cogently presented to demonstrate to the trainee that the question of how to diagnose is truly representative of a host of questions pertaining to the classification of information. One can also clarify for the trainee that a given therapeutic perspective entails the organization of a set of concepts and that all concepts represent viewpoints that further color the observer's view of the world.

For example: if one utilizes the term *diagnosis* in the literal medical sense to mean

a description that pulls together an etiology (a cause), a pathogenesis (the sequence of processes whereby the cause leads to the disease), a syndrome (a collection of symptoms and signs characteristic of illness), and a typical treatment and clinical course. (French, 1977, p. 69)

and then is faced with a family perspective that does not identify clinical disease entities—there is no way to discuss *diagnosis*.

But if the term *diagnosis* (Greek: knowing between) is viewed as having been read in the medical tradition to refer to the clinical determination of individual disease entities (or dysfunction) "employing *categories* drawn from a *system of classification* of diseases" (Prugh, Engel, & Morse, 1975, p. 263)—a nosology—then it becomes apparent that diagnosis relates to classification, and classification relates to the organization of information, and that the basis of all diagnosis rests on the conceptual or informational sets that are called *models* or *therapeutic frameworks*.

It is at this point that the trainee is able to make a leap from a bird's-eye view that diagnosis means relating to a nosology that holds a key to understanding. The trainee can then see that diagnosis relates to a corpus of information (a theoretical perspective), and can understand that for diagnosis to occur, there must indeed be a relationship between the following:

- the body of information or theoretical perspective
- the type of material sought in the psychiatric interview
- the manner in which the information is shaped and classified by the patient and therapist using the theory as a frame of reference
- how the material is used by the therapist to suggest routes of intervention

Thus if students examine family functioning from a *strategic* perspective (Haley, 1980; Madanes, 1981) they may now begin to comprehend that if in this framework a symptom is viewed as a protective solution, by which the symptom-bearer sacrifices himself or herself to sustain a family homeostasis, that the therapist will follow the premises of the viewpoint in gathering data, while employing a notion that symptom presentation is a helpful response by the family as an organization under stress that sustains dysfunction. If the trainee is working under a *structural* family perspective (Minuchin, 1974, Minuchin & Fishman, 1981), the working assumption that will lead to gathering data and defining the meaning of the data will be that this family organism as a complex system is underfunctioning. The underfunctioning will be seen as a result of a malalignment in the family structure (e.g., father is too peripheral to mother and mother and son are overinvolved).

If the novice utilizes an *interactional* perspective (Greenberg, 1977, 1980; Watzlawick et al. 1967, 1977; Weakland et al. 1974) one of the primary theoretical assumptions will be that the problem and symptom formation is a product of what the family members are doing with each other.

Each framework leads to gathering of information along particular theoretical lines and the information obtained is classified in a series of statements pertaining to the nature of the problem or dysfunction—this is the diagnosis or diagnostic assessment. From the diagnostic assessment, the theory if utilized appropriately will suggest a series of intervention pathways. For example, the structuralist's formulation as overly simplified above would suggest that the route of intervention will be focused toward modifying the structural alignments and hence the shape of the structure of the family. The interactional therapist would suggest that as the emerging symptom formation is the outcome of the manner in which family members are dealing with each other that the focus of intervention will be to effect a shift in what they are doing with each other (Greenberg, 1980).

Once again the students may find themselves on the horns of a false dilemma. For often the novice will appropriately conclude that "It's all in a viewpoint," that is, the theoretical stance not only helps to define the meaning and/or perception of the information obtained, but also shapes and defines the language the therapist employs in describing what is observed. However, the error typically made by the trainee is to make a leap from "It's all in a viewpoint" to "Everything is in the viewpoint." When this occurs the student frequently tries to treat the theory and attempts to force all the information into that format, even though no theoretical view can account for all the data obtained.

Here the teacher must continue to remind the student that the theory is but a reference point, and hence a guide for making sense and order out of phenomena. Otherwise the trainees tend to concretize and literalize theory much the same way they attempted to wedge a theoretical perspective under the heading of "diagnosis."

When the trainees are partially successful in moving away from the previously limited meaning of diagnosis, they are ready for an enlarged concept that depicts diagnosis as *a set of statements characterizing individual or family functioning that are derived from basic premises comprising a therapeutic framework or schemata that can be utilized as a frame of reference for making sense and order out of the phenomena that are presented and arises in the therapeutic encounter.* The stage has then been set to begin to effectively gather data along the guidelines of a particular theoretical perspective, as well as to begin to deal with family diagnosis and assessment appropriately.

REFERENCES

American Psychiatric Association. *Diagnostic and statistical manual of mental disorders, DSM III.* Washington, D.C.: Author, 1980.

Bateson, G., Jackson, D., Haley, J., & Weakland, J. Towards a theory of schizophrenia. *Behavioral Science,* 1956, *1,* 251–264.

Bodin, A.M. The interactional view: Family therapy approaches of the Mental Research Institute. In A.S. Burman & D. Kniskern (Eds.), *Handbook of family therapy.* New York: Brunner Mazel, 1981.

Bowen, M. Family therapy after twenty-five years. In M. Bowen (Ed.), *Family therapy in clinical practice.* New York: Aronson, 1978, pp. 285–320.

Ferreira, A. Family myth and homeostasis. *Archives of General Psychiatry,* 1963, *9,* 457–463.

Ferreira, A. Psychosis and family myth. *American Journal of Psychotherapy,* 1967, *21,* 186–197.

French, A.P. *Disturbed children and their families: Innovations in the evaluation and treatment.* New York: Human Science, 1977.

Greenberg, G.S. The family interactional perspective: A study and examination of the work of Don D. Jackson. *Family Process,* 1977, *16,* 358–412.

Greenberg, G.S. Problem-focused brief family interactional psychotherapy. In L.R. Wolberg & M.L. Aronson (Eds.), *Group and family therapy.* New York: Brunner Mazel, 1980.

Haley, J. *Problem solving therapy.* San Francisco: Jossey-Bass, 1976.

Haley, J. *Leaving home: The therapy of disturbed young people.* New York: McGraw-Hill, 1980.

Madanes, C. *Strategic family therapy.* San Francisco: Jossey Bass, 1981.

Minuchin, S. *Families and family therapy.* Cambridge, Mass.: Harvard, 1974.

Minuchin, S., & Fishman, H.C. *Family therapy techniques.* Cambridge, Mass.: Harvard, 1981.

Prugh, D.G., Engel, M., & Morse, W.C. Emotional disturbance in children. In N. Hobbs (Ed.) *Issues in the classification of children.* San Francisco: Jossey-Bass, 1975.

Satir, V. *Conjoint family therapy* (rev. ed.). Palo Alto, Calif.: Science & Behavior, 1967.

Sluzki, E.E., & Ransom, D.C. (Eds.). *Double bind: The foundation of the communicational approach to the family.* New York: Grune & Stratton, 1976.

Watzlawick, P., Beavin, J., & Jackson, D. *Pragmatics of human communication.* New York: Norton, 1967.

Watzlawick, P., & Weakland, J.H. (Eds.). *The interactional view: Studies at the Mental Research Institute, Palo Alto, 1965–1974.* New York: Norton, 1977.

Weakland, J.H., Fisch, R., Watzlawick, P., & Bodin, A.M. Brief therapy: Focused problem resolution. *Family Process,* 1974, *13,* 141–168.

8. The Live Supervision Form: Structure and Theory for Assessment in Live Supervision

Anthony W. Heath, Ph.D.
Director of Supervision and Training
Consultation for Change
Elgin, Illinois

Eight

In 1973, Braulio Montalvo, of the Philadelphia Child Guidance Clinic, published the ideas and details of live supervision. Soon thereafter, one way mirrors and buzzing sound systems were installed in family therapy rooms all over the country, and supervisors and therapists struggled to learn to work together in new ways. Today there is little question that live supervision, which allows supervisors to observe and immediately redirect therapy sessions, has distinct advantages for therapists (Haley, 1976; Kempster & Savitsky, 1967) and for families.

For supervisors though, learning to conduct live supervision was often difficult. Many had to convince therapists that observation of their work could benefit them. Most had to create functional hierarchies in their agencies so that therapists would accept supervisory directives. Everyone had to learn to deliver precise live interventions.

As all of these challenges were conquered, supervisors settled back into their observation rooms and asked themselves a very difficult question: "What shall I say?" Supervisors were tempted to think about sessions as if they were the therapist, and accordingly to suggest therapeutic interventions.

Difficulties often arose when supervisors focused on the *family* as the unit of observation and intervention in supervision. Therapists, directed to do what their supervisors would do, often expressed displeasure with their new roles as puppets. To correct this imbalance some therapists and supervisors agreed to work together as cotherapists, watching each other work from an observation room. Such symmetry or equality in supervisor–therapist relationships worked well except when one of the pair de-

145

sired a more traditional, hierarchical relationship. Every therapist who has wished that his or her supervisor would act like a supervisor knows this difficulty well.

Supervisors can avoid the difficulties encountered in live supervision by thinking of live supervision as a context for therapist skill development rather than as a new method of cotherapy. In thinking this way supervisors consistently focus on the *therapy* as the unit of observation and intervention. Supervisors must observe the interaction between therapist and family, and intervene to change the interaction through the therapist. Thus supervisors help therapists change while therapists help families change.

Supervisors who accept responsibility for helping therapists change have their work cut out for them. First, they must know how to establish parameters for working with therapists during therapy sessions. Second, supervisors must know what to watch for during sessions lest they slip into watching the family rather than the therapist–family interaction. Third, supervisors must know how to organize their observations for maximum immediate and long-range effect. In other words, supervisors must have a way to quickly *assess* the immediate and long-range progress of therapy, so that live interventions will be valuable for the therapist as well as for the family. To date, the literature has contained little advice from the experts on these matters.

In this article, the author will present a live supervision instrument that enables supervisors to organize their ongoing assessment of therapist skills. The Live Supervision Form (Exhibit 8-1) provides a structure for live supervision, reminds supervisors that their work should stress therapist skill development, and allows supervisors to take notes that have immediate and long-range value in supervision.

The Live Supervision Form does not define what supervisors should observe in live supervision, or how or when they should intervene. Guidance on these issues requires a brief and eminently practical discussion of theory in live supervision. Description of the form and instructions for its use in ongoing assessment in live supervision will follow the theory section.

PRACTICAL THEORY IN LIVE SUPERVISION

Live supervision, like family therapy, emerged as "techniques in search of a theory" (Manus, cited in Olson & Sprenkle, 1976, p. 317).

With the published literature on the method lagging behind, supervisors developed their techniques through informal experimentation. Live interventions were used when they seemed appropriate, and notes were taken on anything that seemed important. As supervisors gained experience, they became increasingly self-consistent in their thinking and behavior.

There are no formal theories of family therapy supervision (Everett, 1980), and no formal theories of *live* supervision. This is not to say that supervisors work without theories. Liddle and Halpin (1978) observed that supervisory goals and methods seem to be consistent with the therapy theory of the supervisor. To a greater or lesser extent, supervisors use their ideas about therapy to guide their work as supervisors.

Supervisors can use *family therapy theories* to guide their perceptions, conceptualizations, and interventions during live supervision. This can be a simple process, and it is consistent with the belief that therapy and supervision are isomorphic (Liddle & Saba, 1982). Rather than becoming eclectic in the supervision context and complaining about the lack of live supervision theory, supervisors should attempt to apply their relatively extensive and organized body of knowledge about therapy to supervision. By asking oneself "What would I look for, think, and do right now if the therapist were my client", supervisors will usually become suddenly aware of new options for live supervision.

Supervisors should continually assess the usefulness of their therapy theory as a supervision theory. The fit between the two may be imperfect. Should a therapy idea prove unuseful for supervision, the supervisor should try a different approach. In the author's experience strategic, structural, and functional family therapy theories apply easily to live supervision. Supervisors of other theoretical orientations may find that live supervision is incompatible with their ideas about therapy. For example, a supervisor who prefers to be nondirective as a therapist may be most uncomfortable with the call for direction in live supervision. The author suggests that there is room for change in such a situation.

Supervisors must consistently use their newly formed theories of supervision to conceptualize *supervisory* interventions. Again, the supervisor's "client" is the therapist, and the therapist's client is the family. A supervisor's and a therapist's theoretical orientations do not have to be the same, but supervisors must have a working knowledge of and basic respect for the therapist's approach. Supervisors can then help (according to their supervision theory) each therapist to intervene according to his or her therapy theory. By concentrating one's efforts on skillful supervision, supervisors allow therapists to concentrate on skillful therapy. The complexity of each of the parallel processes warrants this division of labor.

The author has found it extremely valuable to bring his supervision in line with his therapy in the manner described. By using strategic therapy theory as the conceptual basis for assessment in live supervision, new avenues for intervention have seemed to appear as needed.[1] For example, assessment during strategic therapy focuses on identifying clearly defined problems and gathering information on the patterns that maintain them. Strategic interventions attempt to disrupt problem sequences. Applying these ideas to supervision, it becomes clear that supervisors and therapists must agree to work on specific problems, or (to put it more positively) goals. Live interventions and intersession homework assignments (Schwartz, 1982) are therefore designed to interrupt patterns preventing attainment of long- and short-range skill development goals. The Live Supervision Form, described in the next section, has proved useful in the ongoing assessment necessary in strategic supervision.

THE LIVE SUPERVISION FORM

The Live Supervision Form was developed and revised by the author during four years of use in the Marriage and Family Therapy Center of Purdue University. The form was designed for live supervision, and has been used primarily with therapists with structural and/or strategic orientations. Eight supervisors used the form shown in Exhibit 8-1 during the 1981-1982 academic year. The author has also used the form for live supervision and case consultations in community agencies.

The form is printed on two part no carbon required (NCR) paper. The *original* copy is given to the therapist following the postsession meeting. This allows therapists to listen to the supervisor's comments and suggestions (rather than taking notes) and to keep a copy for later review. The *duplicate* is kept in the supervisor's binder for aiding recollection of specific information. Supervisors also find that occasional review of their notes helps to capture patterns in therapists' development.

The form reflects the traditional procedure for live supervision, which includes a *presession* planning conference, *intrasession* assessment and intervention, and a *postsession* debriefing (Heath, 1982). The double lines on the form divide the sections. Description of the form, by section, follows below.

Presession Conference

During the presession conference, supervisors should accomplish four tasks. First, data that identify the session should be filled in, including the date, therapist name, client name or identifier, time of the session, therapy room number, and session number. Second, session objectives should be recorded. These objectives are most useful when they are specific (e.g., to track the sequence leading to abuse) since they can then be used to evaluate the session. Third, the prearranged live intervention format should be completed. This portion of the form allows supervisors and therapists to negotiate the way in which they will work together during the session. Overt agreement on how the supervisor will intervene removes the surprise element from live supervision and it facilitates a sense of cooperation. According to this mini-contract supervisors may agree to direct the therapist by phone, through a bug-in-the ear device (Birchler, 1975), or by walking into the sessions. Supervisors may also call for immediate conferences by knocking on the therapy room door or wait for prearranged intrasession conferences. If the therapist prefers a specific intervention style (i.e., directive or consultative), it can be noted, as can other requests which the therapist makes of observers (Heath, 1982). Fourth, the supervisor may wish to note any of the therapist's long-range skill development goals that will be monitored during the session. Skill development goals are agreed upon by therapist and supervisor early in the supervisory relationship. The theoretical orientation used in the case should be entered so that the supervisor may formulate interventions consistent with the chosen approach. The faculty and students of the Purdue Marriage and Family Therapy Program have found that theories are most useful if used consistently on a case by case basis. Thus a student may work strategically with one case and structurally with another.

Intrasession Assessment and Intervention

During the session, the supervisor must continually assess the progress of the session in relation to the therapist's specific and long-range skill development goals. This assessment is guided by the supervisor's theory of supervision. Supervisors should therefore use the Observations and Comments section of the form to record notes about the therapist–family interaction. These notes may include structural diagrams, descriptions of interactions, hypotheses about interactions, suggestions for alternative approaches, records of live interventions made by the supervisor, and evaluative comments about therapist behavior. The author has found that specific records of session events, when used according to supervisory objectives, are well received by therapists. The notes made during the session may be used in postsession discussions to plan new approaches to the case and to review the therapist's goals. Most supervisors develop shorthand symbols to differentiate among their notations.

Session themes can be noted in the appropriate box on the form. Themes should capture therapist–family interaction over the entire session. Examples of session themes include "therapist joining," "problem definition," "defining father as expert," and "gathering sequential data." Recording themes allows supervisors to recall the broad strokes of therapy from session to session.

Notes taken during the session should complement live interventions. In live supervision, assessment of session progress should be quick and should yield prompt, clear suggestions for change. While beginning supervisors tend to use their time taking notes, experienced supervisors tend to take fewer notes and make more live interventions. The importance of timing in live supervision warrants a brief digression.

A supervisor's theory of supervision offers guidance on the timing of interventions in live supervision. The following guidelines for live intervention reflect the strategic/structural orientation of the group that developed them.[2] According to this orientation, supervisors should intervene in sessions when the therapist:

1. strays from a predefined task for more than a few minutes
2. engages in any more-of-the same interaction including rambling and redundancy
3. responds as a family member rather than as a therapist
4. becomes passive in response to chaos
5. enters a power struggle with a family member
6. delivers an intervention that has elicited an undesirable response

These guidelines are moderately specific and consistent with a strategic/structural orientation. They allow ample room for supervisor judgment.

Near the end of the session supervisors should record the homework (if any) as it was assigned to the family. Again, this will allow supervisors to recall the homework prior to the beginning of the next session. The Next Appointment box is self-explanatory.

Postsession Conference

After the session the supervisor's task is to present a summary of his or her observations and comments and to recommend actions for future sessions. In the author's experience, therapists seem to only benefit from a few "bits" of information (Miller, 1956). Therefore, it behooves supervisors to spend several minutes preparing and prioritizing their comments prior to convening a postsession conference.

Supervisors will approach the postsession conference according to their supervision theories. A strategic supervisor, for example, would want to speak the therapist's language, review progress on case-specific and skill development goals, and assign a task to the therapist. This could easily take 30 minutes. A structural supervisor would probably have been more active during the session, and would have less to say afterwards. In any case, before and during the postsession conference recommendations should be entered on the form for future reference.

If the supervision of the case is to be counted as approved supervision by the American Association for Marriage and Family Therapy, the time involved should be entered in the boxes provided. The supervisor then initials the form and gives the original copy to the therapist. The duplicate is kept by the supervisor.

In summary, the Live Supervision Form is an instrument that can be used to structure the process of live supervision. When used by supervisors with clear theories of supervision, it allows concise records to be kept of the notes taken during live supervision. Review of these records gives supervisors a way to assess long-range progress of families and therapists to supplement the assessment that occurs during therapy sessions.

CONCLUSION

In live supervision supervisors must continually assess the progress of therapy; conceptualize clear, effective interventions; and intervene, all in very short periods of time. To assess, conceptualize, and intervene at the necessary pace, supervisors depend on their theoretical understanding of supervision, and their technical abilities as supervisors. When their theories are practical *and* their techniques graceful, live supervision is at its best.

The technology of live supervision has certainly advanced since Montalvo's (1973) excellent paper first appeared (Coppersmith, 1978;

Exhibit 8-1 The Live Supervision Form

☐ Live Supervision
☐ Case Conference

Date	Therapist	Clients	Time	Room #	Session #

Session Objectives:
1.
2.
3.

Prearranged Live Intervention Format:
☐ Phone-in ☐ Bug in Ear ☐ Knock ☐ Walk-in
☐ Midsession Conference at _____
☐ Specific Intervention Style: _____
☐ Other Requests of Observers:

Observations and Comments:

Therapist's Skill Development Goals and/or Theoretical Orientation:

Session Themes:

Next Appointment:

Day   Date   Time

Homework Assigned:

Summary of Observations and Comments:
1.
2.
3.

Recommendations for Future Sessions:
1.
2.
3.

AAMFT Approved Supervision Credit

☐ ☐ ☐
Hours & Minutes

Supervisor's Initials

Breunlin & Cade, 1981). Unfortunately, theories of live supervision remain obscure. If the field of family therapy is to produce "consistent and integrated training and supervisory models" (Everett, 1980, p. 378), live supervision theory will have to develop significantly.

In this chapter readers have been introduced to an instrument which can be used to organize assessment during live supervision. The content of the assessment, however, must be filled in by the supervisor based on his or her theory of supervision. Through the form the author hopes to challenge front line supervisors to make their theories of supervision as practical as their techniques.

NOTES

1. Readers interested in strategic supervision should see a preliminary paper on the topic by Dr. Cheryl Storm and the author (Storm & Heath, 1982) and more detailed papers now in preparation.
2. These guidelines were developed by Cathy Cyrus, Phil Sutton, Susan Regas, and Chuck Romig during a seminar on live supervision at Purdue University, taught by the author and Cheryl Storm. A similar set of guidelines can be found in a clear, practical article by Bullock and Kobayashi (1978).

REFERENCES

Birchler, G. Live supervision and instant feedback in marriage and family therapy. *Journal of Marriage and Family Counseling*, 1975, *1*, 331–342.

Breunlin, D., & Cade, B. Intervening in family systems with observer messages. *Journal of Marital and Family Therapy*, 1981, *7*, 453–460.

Bullock, D., & Kobayashi, K. The use of live consultation in family therapy. *Family Therapy*, 1978, *5*, 244–250.

Coppersmith, E. Expanding uses of the telephone in family therapy. *Family Process*, 1978, *17*, 225–230.

Everett, C. Supervision of marriage and family therapy. In A. Hess (Ed.), *Psychotherapy supervision: Theory, research, and practice*. New York: Wiley-Interscience, 1980.

Haley, J. *Problem solving therapy*. San Francisco: Jossey-Bass, 1976.

Heath, A. Team family therapy training: Conceptual and pragmatic considerations. *Family Process*, 1982, *21*, 187–194.

Kempster, S., & Savitsky, E. Training family therapists through "live" supervision. In N. Ackerman, F. Beatman, & S. Sherman (Eds.), *Expanding theory and practice in family therapy*. New York: Family Service Association of America, 1967.

Liddle, H., & Halpin, R. Family therapy training and supervision literature: A comparative review. *Journal of Marriage and Family Counseling*, 1978, *4*, 77–98.

Liddle, H., & Saba, G. Teaching family therapy at the introductory level: A model emphasizing a pattern which connects training and therapy. *Journal of Marital and Family Therapy*, 1982, *8*, 63–72.

Miller, G. The magical number seven, plus or minus two: Some limits on our capacity for processing information. *The Psychological Review,* 1956, *63,* 81–97.

Montalvo, B. Aspects of live supervision. *Family Process,* 1973, *12,* 343–359.

Olson, D., & Sprenkle, D. Emerging trends in treating relationships. *Journal of Marriage and Family Counseling,* 1976, *2,* 317–329.

Schwartz, R. The pre-session worksheet as an adjunct to training. *American Journal of Family Therapy,* 1981, *9,* 89–90.

Storm, C., & Heath, A. Strategic supervision? The danger lies in discovery. *The Journal of Strategic and Systemic Therapies,* in press.

9. Ecological Assessment

Bradford P. Keeney, Ph.D.
Director of Research
The Ackerman Institute for Family Therapy
New York, New York

Nine

IN A CLASSIC PAPER ON THE FUTURE OF PERSONALITY measurement, Mischel (1977) proposed that "if human behavior is determined by many interacting variables—both in the person and in the environment—then a focus on any one of them is likely to lead to limited predictions and generalizations" (p. 246). An immediate implication is that clinical investigation should incorporate multi-assessment strategies. Historically, this approach was introduced in the field of psychometrics by Campbell and Fiske (1959) as "Multitrait–Multimethod (MT–MM) matrix analysis." This orientation was subsequently extended to the context of family measurement by Strauss's (1968) suggestion that the ideal empirical situation would be characterized by "develop[ing] measures (or use[ing] existing techniques) for two or more properties using two or more different methods for each of the properties" (p. 337).

This article argues that multiple goals of measurement and the development of multiple measurement strategies in family therapy require an ecological form of assessment. Ecological assessment, as proposed here, suggests that diverse system levels, as well as their relations, be assessed and evaluated. Following Wade (1978), I propose that it is important to distinguish among three basic levels of family system:

1. the behavior and characteristics of individuals
2. social relationships indicated by dyadic interaction
3. social group structures that organize the relations among dyadic interactions

Ecological assessment is therefore most basically aimed at gaining access to information from these diverse system levels.

TOWARD A TYPOLOGY OF FAMILY ASSESSMENT

From the perspective of multiple system levels, a typology of assessment tools and techniques could be initially elaborated that would distinguish measures with regard to their intended level of assessment. For example, a Minnesota Multiphasic Personality Inventory (MMPI) is clearly intended to assess individual characteristics. Other measures focus on dyads (e.g., Hurvitz's Marital Roles Inventory, 1965) or whole social groups (e.g., Kvebaek's Family Sculpting Test, 1973). Cromwell and Keeney (1979) discuss the use of these particular measures to assess different system levels. A classification scheme presented by Cromwell, Olson, and Fournier (1976) distinguished diagnostic tools and techniques in marital and family therapy on the basis of the intended unit of assessment in terms of individual, marital dyad, partial family, and whole family.

Unfortunately, this form of classification only distinguishes the *intended* focus of the measure. It does not distinguish the level of system that responds or is observed during the assessment process. For example, in the case of the Marital Roles Inventory, one has a measure intended to focus on the marital dyad, but the level of system responding is an individual. Ravich's (1969) train game, on the other hand, is a measure focused on the dyadic system and is derived from dyadic interaction.

This distinction brings into awareness an important empirical issue concerning whether (or to what extent) a measure that taps information from an individual level can be used to assess a social relationship or group property. In his review of family measurement, Strauss (1968) noted that "a discipline concerned with groups cannot depend on measurement of the characteristics of individuals or, in most cases, on the summation of the properties of individuals making up the group" (p. 341). He later goes on, however, to observe that most family measures are based on the "aggregation of the characteristics of individuals making up that group." He cites measures of family "religiousness," "maladjustment," and "neuroticism" as examples of this type of indicator.

It could be agreed that forms of description which characterize individuals cannot be used as the basis for depicting social groups. From this perspective assessing each individual in a family for "neuroticism" could not be the basis for a whole family assessment. This sum of the individual scores would be as meaningful as adding the heights of family members and then proposing "family height" as an assessment of a family social property. Sometimes investigators attempt to slide around this slippery approach by speaking of an "average" score, e.g., a family's "average neuroticism" or "average height." This procedure, however, still ignores the systems rule of nonsummativity, which illustrates that the sum of the components is never an adequate representation of the whole.

Of course, there are forms of assessment, based on summing individual measures, that are meaningful. The outcome of an election is one apparent case. For this situation, all individual votes are added and the final tally determines a particular outcome. However, strictly speaking, it is semantically incorrect to say that a *group* elected a leader. More accurately, individuals elected a leader—the group (as a whole entity) never entered a voting booth. This example suggests that efforts to assess whole groups based on individual assessments are a special case of anthropomorphism, i.e., attributing forms of description appropriate to individual systems to a system level of different order.

Much perplexity in social science measurement could be avoided if an ecological awareness prevailed. One major consequence of an ecological view has been stated by Wade: "discussion of or evidence about one level of organization are related to, but not substituted for, discussions of or evidence about another level" (1978, p. 110). A starting point toward ecological assessment is therefore to note the distinction between the level of system that responds or is observed and the system level the investigator using the measure intends to make inferences about. When the level of system tapped does not correspond to the level for which generalizations are sought, it must be remembered that the results obtained will represent only properties of the level tapped. The investigator then steps aside and ponders over what inferences can be made about the relationship of that level of analysis to other system levels.

In spite of the fact that most available measures that claim to assess dyadic interaction and social organization are based on individual assessments, there are instances where the system level assessed corresponds to the level about which inferences are made. On the level of dyadic interaction, the operationalization and typology of forms of dyadic relationship by Sluzki and Beavin (1965) is one example. A more illustrative example of dyadic level of assessment is provided by measures on interpersonal proximity (e.g., Hall, 1969). On the social organization level, some attempts have been made to study whole family interaction (see Riskin and Faunce, 1972, for an evaluative review of family interaction research).

It should be clearly stated at this time that I am not suggesting that measures that tap individuals have no importance for studies primarily concerned with dyadic interaction or group organization. My position is that assessment of individuals is only assessment of the individual level of system. Furthermore, although this information may be used in making inferences about the individual system's *relationship* to dyadic interaction, social organization, or other system levels, it cannot be regarded as representative of these other levels. I suggest the term "system validity" to refer to the level of system from which a measure taps information.

Unfortunately, an examination of the growing networks of literature concerned with "social interaction" and "group organization," particularly in the context of child, marital and family investigation, indicates that system levels are often confounded in assessment and inference. In these research areas, assessments of individuals are often used as a basis for inferences about the dyadic relationship(s) or social group(s) of which they are a part.

Sometimes assessment procedures operate by inquiring about an individual's perception of a relationship or group (e.g., asking each member of a marital dyad to respond to questions concerning their relationship). It must be remembered that this information is still tapped from the individual level of system, although the intention of the assessment procedure is often to generate data from which inferences about the dyad can be made.

It is even possible for such a form of assessment to be "doubly confounded." For example, take the case of a husband and wife's attitudes being measured with respect to what behaviors they like and dislike. If these data are used to create discrepancy scores from which inferences about their relationship are made, then a double error potentially enters the investigation. The first error occurs with regard to the mistyping of system assessed (phenomenology of individuals) to the level of system to which the inference is being made (phenomenology of dyadic relationship). Another mistyping occurs with regard to the questions asked of each individual (i.e., each is asked about behavior rather than about their interaction).

Let us take another example. If a mother was interviewed as to what styles of discipline best characterize her practice as well as what typical kinds of behavior her child exhibits in response to her style, the data would also be tapped from the level of an individual respondent. However, such data could be used to make inferences about the relationship between this individual level (mother) to the dyadic level (mother–child interaction). For example, if mother described herself as being firm, reasonable, and direct and her child as being sensitive, understanding, and immediately responsive, we would be able to make an inference about the mother–child dyad as perceived by the mother.

It is important to note that if mother had only been asked about her style of discipline and not about her child's responses to her style, we could make no inference about her perception of the mother–child interaction. In other words, we would have only one side of her view of the relationship, which by definition does not signify the whole relationship. We might also point out that in addition to asking mother about her discipline style and the child's behavior, we could also ask the child to give us data about these areas. The combination of data from these two individual systems would still not be an assessment of interaction, but would be two individuals' perception of their interaction.

Before going on, I should point out that no system level is ever completely independent or autonomous from other system levels in the everyday flow of action. A more correct description of the ecology of behavior would be to talk of *nested systems,* demonstrating that each level of system is embodied by other levels. Thus, individual behavior is simultaneously social behavior from another point of view and vice versa. In other words, an individual is always part of a social context and a social context always implies the inclusion of different individual systems. The interconnectedness of levels of system suggests that information obtained from any level of system can be used to make inferences about the relation of that system to other levels of system. One must remember, however, that we cannot make direct inferences about a system level on the basis of information derived from a different level of system.

Bateson (1972, 1979) has suggested that this issue be discussed in terms of the form of descriptive language used by the investigator. More simply put, he argues that an investigator should use descriptions that correspond to the level of system being assessed. When speaking of individual behavior, one's descriptions should correspond to that level of phenomena logically. On the other hand, descriptions of dyadic interaction or social organization should not use descriptions based on the individual level of system. To characterize a whole family as "motivated" is to mistype an individual form of description with a social organization. Similarly, to call a person a "leader" is to use half of an interactional description ("leader-follower relationship") and thereby confound an inappropriate level of description with the level of phenomena being studied (Watzlawick, Beavin, & Jackson, 1967).

At this point we can begin to see how our previous distinction between level of system assessed and level to which inferences are intended can be discussed in terms of the investigator's use of description. An investigator who seeks information about a dyadic level of system must in the course of his or her operations be using a set of terms appropriate for describing that system level. In a way, this is equivalent to saying that he must tap information from that level of system. In other words, the form of the information (or description) is determined by the level of system responding or observed. By way of analogy, in physics, for example, the language of particles, as well as the techniques used to study them, are not the same as the language and methods for studying waves (or classes of particles).

A delineation of terms and descriptions that are appropriately matched to diverse system levels is beyond the scope of this article. Nevertheless, it is important to realize that one way of examining whether a measure has system validity is to examine the forms of description involved in the measurement and inference processes. Statements about social organization and interaction based on descriptions characterizing individuals, and vice versa, are clearly mistyped.

Assuming that one had a map that clearly delineated descriptions of system levels, one could proceed to match existing assessment tools and techniques to the appropriate forms of description. Thus, for any given assessment technique, one would examine the form of language used to describe what the technique is intended to assess. Is it intended to be a measure of individual characteristics, dyadic interaction, or social organization? Does the description of its goal of measurement match the level of system intended to be assessed? Given these pieces of information, one could then move on to examine the form of language used in the assessment procedure itself. Whether self-report or observational, what is the level of system corresponding to the form of language in which the results are recorded? Finally, the level of system that responds or is observed in the assessment procedure can be evaluated. With these forms of information, one could determine the extent of the assessment's system validity. In this way, one may delineate the system levels to which inferences can be made given the gleaned information.

TEMPORAL ORDERING OF DATA

Beyond the correct matching of system levels (across forms of description, unit responding or observed, and inferences) ecological assessment is concerned with the ways in which an investigator orders information from system levels, whether between different systems of the same level or across different levels of systems. Historically, most social science has based its research on diachronic ordering of the variables studied. In this way, historical (antecedent) events are examined as to their possible relationships with contemporary (consequent) events. An association between such temporally separate events may lead to proposing a hypothesis of causal connection between the two. This hypothesis of causality, however, is always arbitrarily assumed by the investigator and is not founded upon an empirical or rational basis. As Whitehead (1925, p. 4) points out, since the time of Hume the rationality of science has been denied due to the fact that "the cause in itself discloses no information as to the effect, so that the first invention of it must be *entirely* arbitrary . . ." Science is possible, he argues, because we go ahead and establish "*entirely arbitrary* connections which are not warranted by anything intrinsic to the natures either of causes or effects."

In accordance with this type of temporal ordering of data, ecological assessment suggests that predictions can be proposed within and across different system levels. For example, one might ask whether a particular change in an individual would lead to a particular social organizational change. Can a shift in social organization lead to variation in dyadic interaction? Or, can change in one subsystem of an individual (e.g., biochemical) lead to change in another subsystem of that individual (e.g., behavior)?

Lamb (1979) proposes that anyone investigating social interactional levels must deal with the timing and sequence of the interactants' behaviors. This means, for example, that frequency counts of target behaviors are not acceptable on this level of analysis for they do not provide interactional data. One of the ways in which social interaction has been assessed in order to capture sequence involves the computation of contingent probabilities. These are statements regarding the probability that a given behavior by A will be followed by a given behavior by B. This form of analysis has led to an ability to detect cyclical interaction of variables on dyadic levels. For example, Kendon (1967) has reported that a person's gaze and gaze aversion cycles during conversation intersect like sine and cosine waves. Similarly, Brazelton, Yogman, Als, and Tronick (1979) found that parent–child interaction can be described in terms of interacting cycles.

In contradistinction to diachronic forms of ordering data, there is a synchronic form of ordering data. In the history of science, it can be observed that this perspective emerged partly from the formal study of nonlinear (or synchronic) time and control known as "cybernetics." In brief, a cybernetic form of analysis is one that focuses on how the behavior of a system can be accounted for by its present form of interaction.

For example, there are two ways to account for the running of an automobile engine. One could say that the engine runs because historically someone got into the car and turned the ignition key. The antecedent event of the key turning is diachronically linked to the outcome of the engine operating. Another form of explanation suggests that the engine's running can be accounted for by the simultaneous interaction of all its components.

This latter view takes into account all bits of description of the operating engine (e.g., a governor regulating a flywheel, the gasoline and oil being disseminated to various parts, spark plugs igniting fuel, and so on). Rather than organize these events into a lineal form of sequence, cybernetics concerns itself with a present-state circular description. Therefore, all these events occur simultaneously (and they do, if one examines an operating engine) and are viewed holistically. From this circular or cybernetic definition of causality, any separation of the events into antecedent and consequent events is entirely arbitrary. The formal operations of cybernetics enable one to generate forms of description that capture the wholeness of these interacting systems.

In the field of family therapy this perspective was advocated by Don Jackson (1965) and has more recently become known as the "interactional view" (Watzlawick & Weakland, 1977). Jackson's approach involved observing redundancies in what the family system does in order to derive the rules for the system's particular interactional game. Metaphorically, Jackson was concerned exclusively with the family dance (i.e., the rules of choreography) and was not interested in examining specifics related to the dancers. Changes over lineal time are usually described on the level of changes in the interactional dance, and seldom on the level concerning the lineal ordering of components of the family system.

Jackson's approach demonstrates the cybernetic perspective of nonlineal synchronic time where events (past, present and future) are recorded as if they were simultaneous. In a way, the observer juggles past and future to collapse upon the present. What one obtains within this temporal manipulation is a record of *pattern*. For example, if one continuously traces onto paper the movement of a person's eyes while the person is scanning a picture, a sketch can be derived showing a unique eye scanning pattern (Noton & Stark, 1971). Of course, a continued assessment of these whole patterns over lineal time might indicate changes in scanning patterns.

The objective of the synchronic level of data analysis can therefore be stated as the pursuit of recognizing or deriving patterns in the phenomena of interest. In this regard, it is helpful to remember that one of the consequences of effective measuring instruments is that they enable us to enlarge or reduce our unit of observation such that pattern can be discerned. For example, aim a telescope into the sky and a random scatter plot of stars may appear as the pattern of a spiral galaxy. On another level, an electron scanning microscope enables one to see patterns in the realm of the incredibly minute.

Although this discussion has distinguished diachronic (lineal) and synchronic (nonlineal) temporal orderings of data, I would now like to propose that all assessment strategies simultaneously work on these two levels of temporal ordering. This first of all means that what an investigator identifies as a "unit of analysis" refers to a synchronic ordering of data. The idea of a "unit" presupposes a whole that is fixed in time. In the view of linguists, the word "chair," for example, is actually a label to capture a synchronic ordering of ever changing components (millions of molecules). Since "chairs" change slowly relative to our temporal frame of reference, we can for all practical purposes assume that they are constant. A more formal way of saying this is that although the world most basically is in a Heraclitean flux, observers perceive constancy when sufficiently different orders of change or temporal frames encounter one another.

In family social science, the units of analysis include bits of behavior, behavioral sequences, dyadic interactions, and forms of social organization. All of these expressions capture or represent synchronic patterns of process. Once a unit or synchronic pattern is identified, the investigator then can examine changes of this pattern over lineal or diachronic time. Consequently, the problem of assessment in family therapy (as well as in all of science) initially involves finding a way to discern the unit of analysis one is interested in. Historically, science has progressed through the invention of tools and techniques that enable the observer to gain access to patterns previously unobtainable. The examples of telescopes and microscopes indicated a way to achieve this goal through reduction or magnification of the spatial field of view.

In the social sciences, units of pattern have also been identified through recording the topography wherein phenomena take place. On a microbehavioral level we have mentioned the detection of eye scanning patterns through the use of optical and mechanical recording apparatus. On a macrolevel, Barker's (1968) studies of the ecology of behavior have provided a way of mapping gross patterns of behavior in their social contexts.

In addition to reducing or magnifying the territorial or spatial events upon which phenomena occur, one can change the time frame wherein events are observed in order to detect pattern. An example of this approach is given by the cultural anthropologist Hall (1977, pp. 76–77) who describes the use of film technology in a research project of one of his students:

> Using an abandoned car as a blind, he photographed children dancing and skipping in a school playground during their lunch hour. At first, they looked like so many kids each doing his own thing. After a while, we noticed that one little girl was moving more than the rest. Careful study revealed that she covered the entire playground. Following procedures laid down for my students, this young man viewed the film over and over at different speeds. Gradually, he perceived that the whole group was moving in synchrony to a definite rhythm. The most active child, the one who moved the most, was the director, the orchestrator of the playground rhythm!

The point of these examples is to illustrate that certain forms of synchronic patterns of phenomena (i.e., units of analysis) are detectable to the observer only through manipulating their representation in space and time. The only patterns most observers can detect, without instruments to change their frame of reference, are on the level of discrete behavior. For example, behaviorists are often eager to demonstrate the ease with which their unit of analysis can be discerned and consequently quantified. What is overlooked is that discrete behavioral units appear as "units" (i.e., synchronic patterns) without the aid of intermediary transducers because of the particular relation between temporal frames of the observer and the observed.

Take the example of an undergraduate student pecking a button in order to get a pellet of extra grade points. The pushing of the button is a discrete unit of analysis that can be characterized by an observer as happening or not happening at any moment in time. If one could imagine an observer being on the level of muscle and nerve tissue, the attained observations would be very different. At that level only movement of musculature would be apparent. Here an investigator might choose tendon displacement as a unit of analysis since whether a tendon got displaced or not would be easily observable. What is important to realize is that the larger pattern of an organism pushing a button would be beyond the reach of the observer at this imaginary level of analysis.

The same problem comes into play whenever an unaided investigator seeks to examine a unit of analysis that is not in the same frame of reference as discrete units of behavior. The dilemma of studying dyadic interactional and social organizational levels may not be so much with the slippery abstraction of the concepts utilized as it is with finding a way to detect synchronic patterns at those levels. This discussion suggests that access to units of analysis at these levels requires intermediary transducers or instruments capable of altering the spatial and/or temporal frames within which phenomena occur.

In closing it must be emphasized that ecology, in its most basic meaning, attempts to illuminate the relations within and across diverse levels of a whole ecosystem. Therefore, the final goal of ecological assessment in social science would be to incorporate all levels of analysis. Menzel (1979) similarly argues that

> no theory of behavior can be considered complete unless it can not only deal with several levels of analysis simultaneously but also zoom in almost continuous fashion from one to the other without losing sight of either subject or going out of focus. (p. 300)

The challenge of family social science today can be characterized as not only a search for more sophisticated instrumentation, method and language, but a reach for an appropriate ecological view (Keeney, 1979).

This article has attempted to contribute in this direction by drawing attention to several basic considerations underlying what has been called *ecological assessment.* And lastly, we should remember that the final goal of any science, although probably unobtainable, is to achieve a unified theory. In the domain of social science, ecology becomes the broadest metaphor to signify such an ideal.

REFERENCES

Barker, R.G. *Ecological psychology.* Stanford, Calif.: Stanford University Press, 1968.

Bateson, G. *Steps to an ecology of mind.* New York: Ballantine, 1972.

Bateson, G. *Mind and nature: A necessary unity.* New York: Dutton, 1979.

Brazelton, T.B., Yogman, M., Als, H., & Tronick, E. The infant as a focus for family reciprocity. In M. Lewis and L. Rosenblum (Eds.), *The child and its family.* New York: Plenum Press, 1979.

Campbell, D.T., & Fiske, D.W. Convergent and discriminate validation by the multitrait-multimethod matrix. *Psychological Bulletin,* 1959, *56,* 81-105.

Cromwell, R.E., & Keeney, B.P. Diagnosing marital and family systems: A training model. *The Family Coordinator,* 1979, *28,* 101-108.

Cromwell, R.E., Olson, D.H., & Fournier, D. Tools and techniques for diagnosis in marital and family therapy. *Family Process,* 1976, *15,* 1-50.

Hall, E.T. *The hidden dimension.* New York: Anchor, 1969.

Hall, E.T. *Beyond culture.* New York: Anchor, 1977.

Hurvitz, N. Marital roles inventory as a counseling instrument. *Journal of Marriage and the Family,* 1965, *27,* 492-501.

Jackson, D. The study of the family. *Family Process,* 1965, *4,* 1-20.

Keeney, B.P. Ecosystemic epistemology: An alternative paradigm for diagnosis. *Family Process,* 1979, *18,* 117-129.

Kendon, A. Some functions of gaze direction in social interaction. *Acta Psychologica,* 1967, *26,* 1-47.

Kvebaek, O. Sculpture test: A diagnostic aid in family therapy. Unpublished technical report, Modum Bads Nervesanatorium, Vikersund, Norway, 1973.

Lamb, M.E. Issues in the study of social interaction: An introduction. In M.E. Lamb, S.J. Suomi, & G. Stephenson (Eds.), *Social interaction analysis: Methodological issues.* Madison: The University of Wisconsin Press, 1979.

Menzel, E. General discussion of the methodological problems involved in the study of social interaction. In M.E. Lamb, S.J. Suomi, & G. Stephenson (Eds.), *Social interaction analysis: Methodological issues.* Madison: The University of Wisconsin Press, 1979.

Mischel, W. On the future of personality measurement. *American Psychologist,* 1977, *32,* 246-254.

Noton, D., & Stark, L. Scanpaths in eye movements during pattern perception. *Science,* 1971, *171,* 308-311.

Ravich, R. The use of an interpersonal game-test in conjoint marital psychotherapy. *American Journal of Psychotherapy,* 1969, *23,* 217-229

Riskin, J.M., & Faunce, E.E. An evaluative review of family interaction research. *Family Process,* 1972, *11,* 365–456.

Sluzki, C.E., & Beavin, J. Symmetry and complementarity: An operational definition and typology of dyads. *Acta Psiquiátrica y Psicológica de América Latina,* 1965, *11,* 321–330.

Strauss, M.A. Measuring families. In H.T. Christensen (Ed.), *Handbook of marriage and the family.* Chicago: Rand McNally, 1968.

Wade, T D. Status and hierarchy in nonhuman primate societies. In P.P.G. Bateson & P.H. Klopfer (Eds.), *Perspectives in ethology: Social behavior.* New York: Plenum Press, 1978.

Watzlawick, P., Beavin, J., & Jackson, D. *Pragmatics of human communication.* New York: Norton, 1967.

Watzlawick, P., & Weakland, J.H. *The interactional view.* New York: Norton, 1977.

Whitehead, A.N. *Science and the modern world.* New York: The Free Press, 1925.

10. The Diagnostician

Phoebe Prosky
The Ackerman Institute for Family Therapy
New York, New York

Ten

THERE WAS A CHINESE MAN OF SCIENCE WHO WORE HIS HAIR IN a yunishna* to symbolize his superior intellect. He was in the habit of going for long walks, and as he walked, the animals would all gather around him and he would tell them wonderful stories. One day, he came to a man in great distress. He wished to ease his torment. He searched among the many theories which he had mastered for the understanding of human behavior, but none was quite right for capturing the odd acts of the man, and all fell short of helping him in the least. The man of science was perturbed and sat down on a rock to collect himself. An owl who had accompanied him swooped down from a branch above and, in seven plucks, clipped off the man's yunishna, rendering him like all the other animals. The man of science reached up in astonishment to feel the place where his yunishna had been, but before his hand could reach his head he was struck with an understanding of the man writhing before him. However, he found himself perfectly incapable of putting it into words. As he struggled, the owl suddenly swooped down again and replaced the yunishna. The man of science found words tumbling from his lips, and these words reached the distressed man and calmed him measurably. The man of science carefully removed his yunishna and wrapped it in a bit of cloth. He placed it in his pocket and from that day forward used it only after first seeing with his short hair.

Moral: He sees best who first resumes his animal nature.

*A knot of hair, common to representations of oriental deities, to hold their superior intelligence.

COMMENTARY

The observer affects the observed. We have two types of mental processing, which we ordinarily use together: the digital and the analogic (Bateson, 1972). The analogic processing is the reception of the data by our senses and the awareness of it *in its own terms*. It is a processing we share with the other animals. The digital processing is the translation of the data into words and numbers and the manipulation of it into categories and valuations. It is a processing that sets humans apart from the other animals. The Western search for objectivity has been an attempt to keep the observer out of the observed by highly structuring the digital and the observed (by limiting the variables). We more closely approach objective observation if we quiet the digital functioning of the observer altogether and render him simply receptive. Then he is in the most objective observing state available to consciousness.

In ordinary parlance we have stripped the observer of rational, "objective" functioning, but in fact, it is his pure observational capacity, that which we usually call subjective, which receives information most faithfully. So in fact an observer at his most completely subjective (analogic) is at his most objective in terms of faithful information receptivity.

The process by which an observer becomes completely subjective, observational, and analogic is through engagement in repetitious activity, such as meditation or jogging. This activity functions to eliminate differences in the perceptual field and it therefore eliminates the material with which the digital function operates. The digital function shuts down, deprived of difference, and the analogic continues to function. With practice at maintaining this state, one can quiet the digital function while processing information from the field analogically, purely receptively. The data is still influenced by the nature of the senses, but this state is more nearly objective than that attained by an attempt at structuring both the observed and the digital functioning, as is the case in traditional objective observation.

In the process of diagnosis, we are attempting to perceive another person accurately. In keeping with the formulation above, the most accurate observational stance would be a purely analogic consciousness. If we diagnose from that consciousness, we arrive at a kind of pattern perception of the other person's functioning, which we can then translate into descriptive words (digital terms). This process prevents our bringing our frames of reference to the observational process, and reserves their utilization for the stage of processing following the reception of the data. This greatly reduces contamination by the observer.

REFERENCE

Bateson, G. *Steps to an ecology of mind.* New York: Ballantine, 1972

Index to Collections 1-4

P

R